A BIBLIOGRAPHY OF
THE ARCHEOLOGY OF SOUTHWESTERN
COLORADO:
ARCHULETA, DOLORES, LA PLATA, AND
MONTEZUMA COUNTIES

by
Deborah A. Hull and Douglas D. Scott

Colorado State Office
Bureau of Land Management
1978

FOREWORD

Cultural resource management in the Bureau of Land Management necessitates an understanding of what approaches have been taken in archeology in previous years in order to evaluate cultural values and the steps necessary to protect them. In line with this need to know what has been done, the Bureau is developing a class I inventory or an overview of the archeology on public lands.

It is becoming obvious from our efforts to gather this overview data that in some areas, particularly southwestern Colorado, much of the early archeology which has defined cultural sequences was a result of work done on public lands. In fact, the first two archeological sites recorded in what is now Colorado (the Escalante Site and Canyon Pintado) are on public lands. These sites were recorded in 1776 by Fathers Dominguez and Escalante.

This bibliography is a part of an overview of southwestern Colorado that is still in preparation and encompasses the early work in that portion of the State. In view of the increasing levels of archeological work in southwestern Colorado, particularly in the Bureau of Reclamation's Dolores River Project area, this comprehensive bibliography is being presented so that it may be used to locate often obscure and rare references for those working in the area. The Bureau and other agencies can also utilize this data for their planning and management efforts that require archeological input. It will aid in the search for the pertinent literature that is required for these types of documents and plans. This work is also the first attempt since the 1950's to assemble and update as much of the literature on this subject as was possible.

I am pleased to make this fifth publication in cultural resources available to the public and to the professional community.

DALE R. ANDRUS
State Director
Colorado
Bureau of Land Management

i

TABLE OF CONTENTS

LIST OF FIGURES

ACKNOWLEDGEMENTS

As in any work of this sort, a great many people have aided the endeavor. The authors wish to express their thanks to these individuals for their help and encouragement. Several people deserve special thanks for they have given much of their time to aid in the initial data gathering and review of the first draft of the bibliography. These individuals are: Dr. David A. Breternitz, Dr. Jack Smith, Gary Matlock, Dr. Steve Sigstad, Dr. Bruce Rippeteau and staff, Dr. E. Charles Adams, Dr. Alexander J. Lindsay, Ron Switzer, Gilbert Wenger, and Earl Ingmanson. To these people our sincere thanks for the cooperation and aid that was given.

Jean Jetley, Nancy Frigetto, and Dolores Ripplinger deserve special thanks for their efforts in typing the bibliography and for not complaining about transcribing the hieroglyphics of the authors.

Special thanks goes to Signa Larralde for editing the final manuscript. The bibliography was greatly improved as a result of her efforts.

Leigh Wellborn provided the graphic design for this and previous series publications.

INTRODUCTION

The bibliography is the culmination of six months of intensive research on the archeological literature of southwestern Colorado by the senior author. This research will eventually result in an overview of the prehistory of the Mesa Verde culture area within the bounds of Colorado. Since the final result is still in preparation and the amount of archeological research in the area is increasing, the authors believe this work will serve as an interim guide to the incredible amount of literature on the area. Every effort has been made to diligently search past and current works on southwestern Colorado and cross-reference other bibliographies. The result has been the compilation of over 1,000 references on the archeology of southwestern Colorado. The authors believe this is the most exhaustive search of its kind since Herb Dick's work in the early 1950's (Dick 1953). This bibliography is up-to-date as of January 1978 with a few additional references added since that date.

Undoubtedly there have been sources or literature missed. It is hoped that what was inadvertently overlooked is not a major work. It might be noted that during the course of this research the authors learned of a number of student papers done as a part of some graduate or undergraduate level course that may be useful to the profession. An attempt has been made to cite these works, but many more have probably been missed. Should any work or works have been overlooked, the authors would greatly appreciate any additional data the reader may have available. Any additional references that can be provided will be utilized in the final overview report.

As one reads or even thumbs through the bibliography, it will become apparent that the work mirrors the evolutionary trend that American archeology has taken. The progression from the early theorizing about origins through data gathering and presentation and finally into the current level of sophisticated presentation of data and explanation can easily be seen in the citations.

Although the purpose of this introduction is not to write the history of the Mesa Verde area archeology at this time, it is further worth noting that some of the "father" figures of modern anthropological theory have contributed to the varied literature in this bibliography. Many of the first generation American archeologists, particularly south-westerners, have also contributed to the cited literature. The list of early authors reads something like a Who's Who in Southwest archeology. Names like Holmes, Jackson, Morgan, Wetherill, Nordenskiold, Cummings, Chapin, Hewett, Prudden, Fewkes, Kidder, Morley, Morris, Martin, and Roberts appear in the following pages. Much of the work done by these individuals and others stands the test of time and is still acceptable by today's standards. No small amount of the work of this early period stands alone as the only literature on the subject to date. Again, the purpose here is not to write a history, as that will be a major part of the overview, but rather to disseminate this rather impressive biblio-graphy to the professional community and other interested parties.

BIBLIOGRAPHY

Abel, Leland J.
    1955   San Juan Red Ware, Mesa Verde Gray Ware, Mesa Verde
                  White Ware, and San Juan White Ware. In Pottery
                  types of the Southwest, edited by Harold S. Colton.
                  Museum of Northern Arizona, Ceramic Series 3B.

Adams, E. Charles
    1973a   Hypothesis formulation concerning strategy in site
                  location employed by prehistoric inhabitants of the
                  Upper San Juan Region, Piedra District. Department
                  of Anthropology, University of Colorado, Boulder.
                  xeroxed.

    1973b   Report on 1973 inventory of archaeological resources,
                  Southern Ute Tribe Reservation, Bureau of Indian
                  Affairs. Bureau of Indian Affairs, Ignacio. xeroxed.

    1974   Location strategy employed by prehistoric inhabitants
                  of the Piedra District, Colorado. Southwestern Lore
                  40(1):13-26.

    1975   Causes of prehistoric settlement systems in the lower
                  Piedra District, Colorado. Unpublished Ph.D. disser-
                  tation. Department of Anthropology, University of
                  Colorado, Boulder.

    1976   Locations on some Navajo refugee period sites in
                  Southwest Colorado. Awanyu 4(2):23-30.

Adkins, Frank
    1975   Basketmaker II. All Points Bulletin, Denver Chapter,
                  Colorado Archaeological Society Newsletter 12(7).

Afton, Jean
    1971   Cultural analysis of burial goods from certain Anasazi
                  sites. Southwestern Lore 37(1):15-26.

Ambler, J. Richard
    1977   The Anasazi. Museum of Northern Arizona, Flagstaff.

Amsden, Charles Avery
    1938   The ancient Basketmakers I. Masterkey 12:205-214.

    1939   The ancient Basketmakers II. Masterkey 13:18-25,
                  46-105, 125-131.

1949   Prehistoric Southwesterners from Basketmaker to Pueblo. Southwest Museum, Los Angeles.

Anderson, Bruce A.
1970   A Basketmaker II burial from Archuleta County, Colorado. Southwestern Lore 36(2):34-40.

Anderson, Elaine
n.d.   Fauna. In The Durango South Project: archaeological salvage of two late Basketmaker II sites in the Durango District, by John D. Gooding. Colorado Archaeological Society, Memoir (In press, ms. 1977).

Anderson, Sidney
1961   Mammals of Mesa Verde National Park, Colorado. University of Kansas Museum of Natural History, Monograph 14(3).

Anonymous
1890   Cliff Dweller relics. American Antiquarian 12(43):45.

1893   The Cliff Dwellers. Chicago World's Columbian Exposition, the M. Jay Smith Exploring Co., Chicago.

1908   Our relics in the Mesa Verde. Travel 13:198. New York.

1909a   The Spruce Tree House of the Mesa Verde. Travel 1.

1909b   The Mesa Verde National Park. Press of Charles Scribner's Sons, New York.

1909c   The Spruce Tree House of the Mesa Verde. Popular Science Monthly 75:618-620.

1910   Mesa Verde National Park. In American Scenic and Historical Preservation Society, 15th Annual Report: 126-127. New York.

1915   The Mesa Verde National Park. Press of Charles Scribner's Sons, New York.

1916a   The Mesa Verde National Park. Special characteristic: prehistoric cliff dwellings. In American Scenic and Historical Preservation Society, 21st Annual Report: 668-672. New York.

1916b   American's most marvelous prehistoric ruins. Capitol Life Record 2:2, 6-7, 9, 11, 13, 15. Washington, D.C.

1916c   Ruins of the Mesa Verde National Park. _Science Monthly_ 2:308-212. London.

1917a   America's park of prehistoric ruins. _American Traveller's Gazette_ 67:4-6. New York.

1917b   The Mesa Verde. _Pan American Union_, _Bulletin_ 45: 230-241. Washington, D. C.

1917c   Prehistoric ruins of the Mesa Verde National Park. _Scientific American Supplement_ 83:297. New York.

1919   Delving into how we came to know of the mysterious dwellings in Mesa Verde National Park. _Railroad Red Book_ 35:28-33. Denver.

1920   Hovenweep National Monument proclaimed. In _American Scenic and Historical Preservation Society_, _28th Annual Report_:174-175. New York.

1921a   The archaeological expedition. _University of Denver_, _Bulletin_ 22.

1921b   Excavating cliff dwellings in Mesa Verde. Unique structural features of the kivas of Square Tower House and the discovery of new ruins. _Scientific American Monthly_ 3:9-13.

1923   Basketmaker caves in the Mesa Verde. _El Palacio_ 40(10): 164-165.

1925a   Hovenweep National Monument. In _American Scenic and Historical Preservation Society_, _30th Annual Report_: 144-145. New York.

1925b   Mesa Verde National Park. In _American Scenic and Historical Preservation Society_, _30th Annual Report_:145-156. New York.

1925c   Mesa Verde National Park. _Municipal Facts_ 8:22. New York.

1925d   Yucca House National Monument. _American Scenic and Historical Preservation Society_, _30th Annual Report_: 147-148. New York.

1927   Prehistoric Indian pottery is found in ruins near Mesa Verde, Colorado. _American Indian_ 1(9):8. Tulsa.

1928   Bird fetish from Mesa Verde. El Palacio 45(2):25-29.

1929   Discovery of Mesa Verde Cliff House. Mazama 11:12. Portland, Oregon.

1933   Funds granted for repairs at Mesa Verde and Aztec Ruins. Museum News 11(11):1.

1937   Excavations begun on sites in southwestern Colorado. Field Museum News 1(9):2.

1950   River basin surveys in Colorado. Southwestern Lore 16:13-15.

1959   Checklist of birds of Mesa Verde National Park, Colorado. Mesa Verde National Park Museum, Colorado. mimeographed.

Applegarth, Susan
1974   Survey of the Bayfield-Pagosa Transmission Line. Southwestern Lore 40(314):99-102.

Arrhenuis, Gustaf and Enrico Bonath
1965   The Mesa Verde Loess. In Contributions of the Wetherill Mesa Archaeological Project, assembled by Douglas Osbourne. Society for American Archaeology, Memoir 19:92-101.

Armstrong, D. M.
1972   Distribution of mammals in Colorado. University of Kansas Museum of Natural History, Monograph 3.

Atwood, Wallace W.
1912   A geographic study of the Mesa Verde. Association of American Geographers, Annals 1:95-100.

Atwood, Wallace W. and Kirtley F. Mather
1932   Physiology and Quaternary geology of the San Juan Mountains, Colorado. U.S. Geological Survey, Professional Paper 166.

B. W. H.
1882   Aztec remains in La Plata County Colorado. Kansas City Review 6(7):442.

1890   Cliff Dweller relics, Colorado. American Antiquarian 12(1):43-45.

Baars, Donald L.
1971   The San Juan corner. The Enchanted Wilderness 1:22.

Bailey, A. M. and R. J. Niedrach
    1965   Birds of Colorado, 2 Vols. Denver Museum of Natural
              History, Denver.

Baldwin, Gordon C.
    1938   Basketmaker and Pueblo sandals. Southwestern Lore
              4(1):1-6.

    1963   The Ancient Ones: Basketmakers and Cliff Dwellers of
              the Southwest. Norton, New York.

Barber, E. A.
    1876a   Rock inscriptions of the "ancient Pueblos" of Colorado.
              American Naturalist 10:716-725.

    1876b   Ancient pottery of Colorado, Utah, Arizona and New
              Mexico. American Naturalist 10(8):449-464.

    1877   Stone implements and ornaments from the ruins of
              Colorado, Utah and Arizona. American Naturalist 11(5):
              264-275.

    1878   The ancient Pueblos, or the ruins of the valley of the
              Rio San Juan. Parts 1 and 2. American Naturalist
              12:614.

Barty, Elizabeth Chesley
    1956   Americans before Columbus. The Viking Press, New York.

Bell, Patti
    n.d.   Microflora and microfauna from the Tamarron Site,
              5LP326. Southwestern Lore (In press, ms. 1977).

Bell, W. H. and E. F. Castetter
    1941   The utilization of yucca, stool, and bear grass by the
              aborigines. University of New Mexico, Biological Series
              5(5).

Bennett, Kenneth A.
    1975   Skeletal remains from Mesa Verde National Park, Colorado.
              National Park Service Wetherill Mesa Studies, 2.

Bennett, Kenneth A. and Frederick S. Hulse
    1966   Micro evolution at Mesa Verde. International Congress
              of Americanists, 36th Proceedings.

Bessels, E.
    1876   The human remains found among the ancient ruins of
              southwestern Colorado and New Mexico. U.S. Geological
              Survey, Bulletin 2:47-63.

5

Birkedal, Terje G.

1968   Site 1926: an isolated Pueblo III kiva near Long House: Wetherill Mesa. In Contributions to Mesa Verde archaeology V, emergency archaeology in Mesa Verde National Park, Colorado, 1948-1966, edited by R. H. Lister. University of Colorado Studies, Series in Anthropology, No. 15.

1970   The manos of Chimney Rock. Paper prepared for anthropology class 520, Dr. Eddy. Department of Anthropology, University of Colorado, Boulder. xeroxed.

1976a   Basketmaker III residence units: a study of prehistoric social organization in the Mesa Verde Archaeological District. Unpublished Ph.D. dissertation. Department of Anthropology, University of Colorado, Boulder.

1976b   Salvage excavations on Wetherill Mesa, Mesa Verde National Park Colorado 1970-71, sites 1937, 1938, 1571, 1940, 1554, 1553, 1824. Mesa Verde National Park, Colorado. xeroxed.

Birksall, W. R.

1891   The cliff dwellings of the canyons of the Mesa Verde. American Antiquarian and American Geographical Society Bulletin 23:584-620.

Bolton, Herbert E.

1972   Pageant in the wilderness. The story of the Escalante Expedition to the interior basin, 1776. Utah State Historical Society, Salt Lake City.

Boyer, W. E.

1928   Customs of Cliff Dwellers. Municipal Facts 11:26. New York.

Bradley, B.

1974   Preliminary excavations at the Wallace Ruin. Southwestern Lore 40(3 and 4):63-71.

Brandagee, T. S.

1876   The flora of southwestern Colorado. United States Geological and Geographic Survey, Bulletin 3(3):227-248.

Breternitz, David A.

1966   An appraisal of tree ring dated pottery types in the Southwest. Anthropological Papers of the University of Arizona, No. 10.

1971   Partial report of inventory of Indian ruins, Dolores
River area. Memorandum report, 1 October 1971. Bureau
of Land Management, Denver. xeroxed.

1972a   Archaeological survey of Mesa Verde National Park,
Long Mesa. 1971. (3 Vols.) Mesa Verde National Park,
Colorado. xeroxed.

1972b   Final report of inventory of Indian ruins, Dolores
River area. Bureau of Land Management, Montrose.
xeroxed.

1973a   Summary of the archaeological survey of a proposed
wilderness area in Mesa Verde National Park. Mesa
Verde National Park, Colorado. xeroxed.

1973b   Tree ring dated Basketmaker III and Pueblo 1 sites in
Mesa Verde National Park. Midwest Archaeological Center,
National Park Service, Lincoln. xeroxed.

1974   Archaeological resources of the McPhee Reservoir area.
Dolores River Project. Bureau of Reclamation, Durango.
xeroxed.

1975a   Archaeological resources of the Towaoc Canal and
laterals, Dolores River Project, Colorado. National
Park Service Interagency Archaeological Services,
Denver. xeroxed.

1975b   Cultural resource inventory of the Kiva Point Locality,
Ute Mountain, Ute Homeland. Bureau of Indian Affairs,
Albuquerque. xeroxed.

1975c   Mesa Verde Research Center, 1975. <u>Southwestern Lore</u>
41(4):17-21.

1975d   Summary of archaeological resources, Dolores River
Project, southwest Colorado. Midwest Archaeological
Center, National Park Service, Lincoln. xeroxed.

Breternitz, David, Terje Birkedal, and Dan Martin
    1971   The archaeological survey of Mesa Verde National Park,
Long Mesa, Vols. 1 and 2, parts 1-4. Mesa Verde National
Park, Colorado. xeroxed.

Breternitz, David A. and Jack Smith
    1972   Mesa Verde; the green table. In <u>National parkways</u>.
Worldwide Research and Publishing Company, Casper.

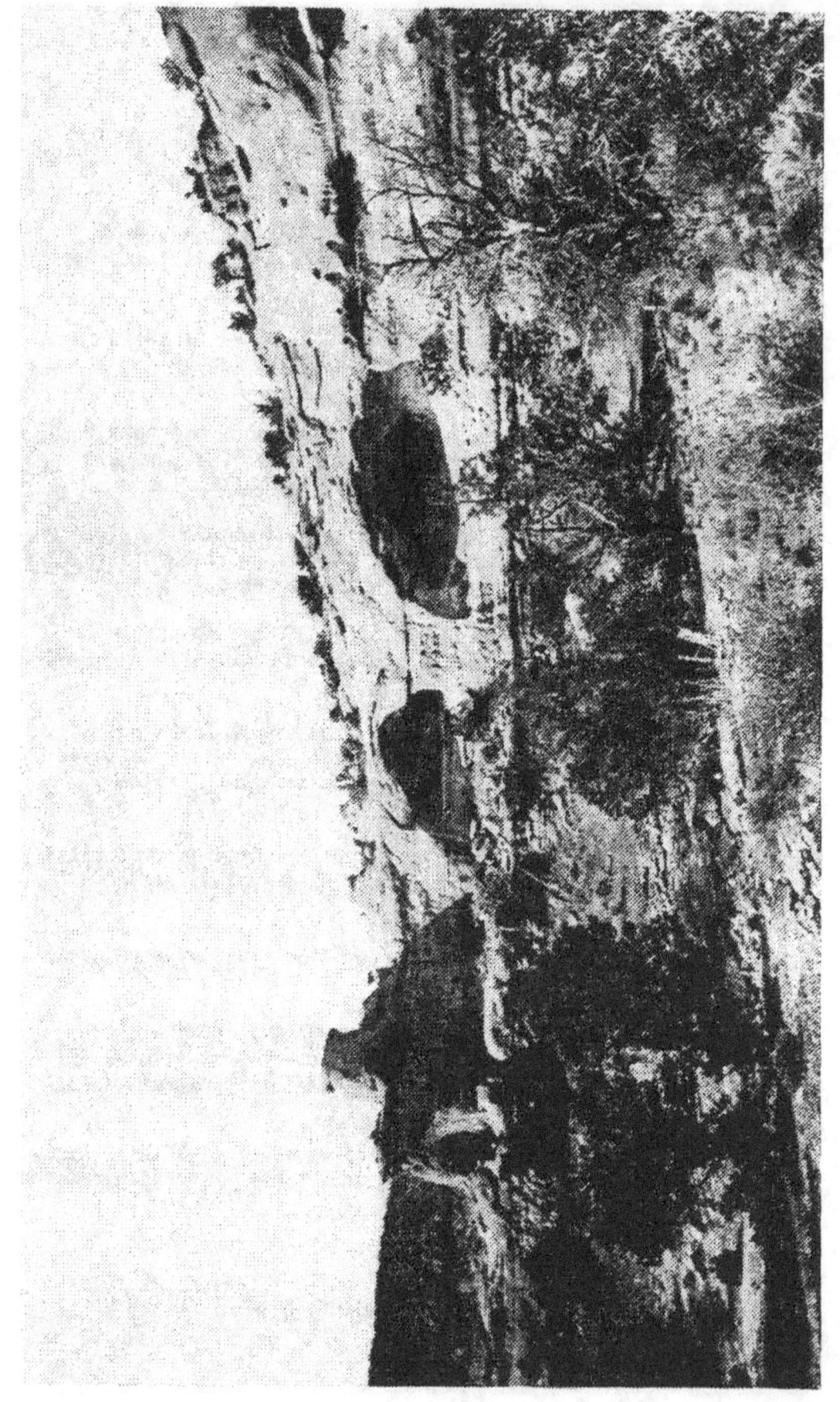

FIGURE 1. Circa 1875 photograph of cliff dwelling in Sand Canyon by W. H. Jackson. Courtesy Smithsonian Institution National Anthropological Archives.

8

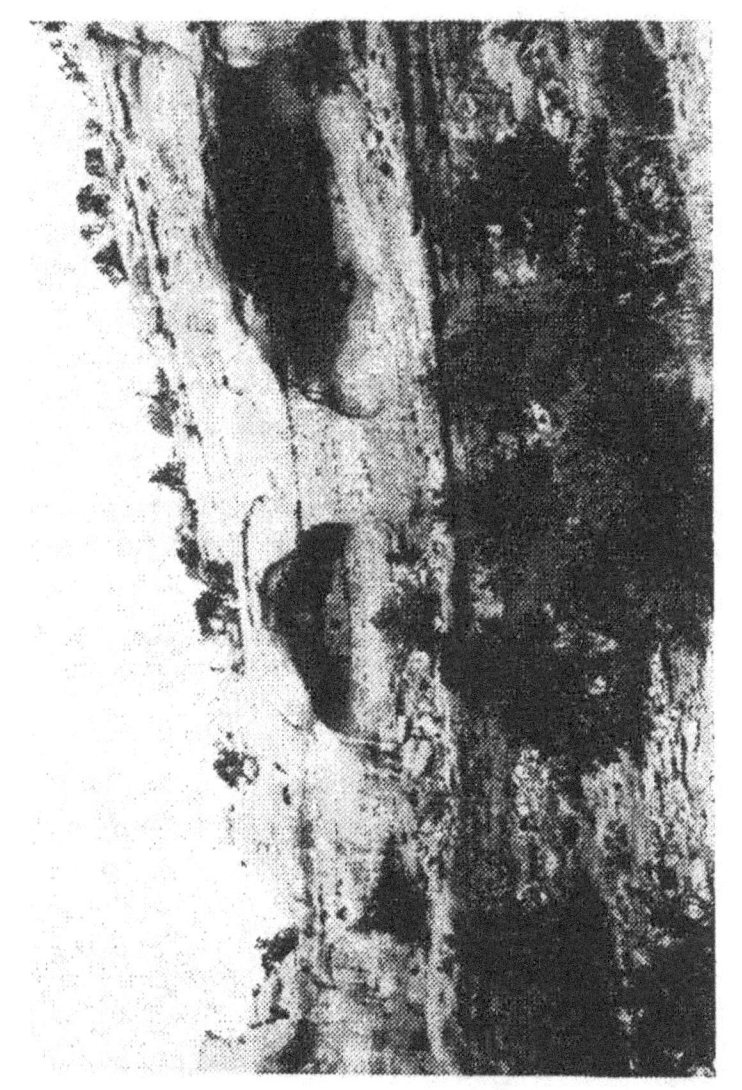

FIGURE 2. 1977 photograph of 5MT 1828.
This view of the same site as Figure 1 shows the lack of
destruction to isolated sites and the extraordinary
preservation qualities of rock shelters. Note the lack
of change in the vegetation over a 100-year period.

Breternitz, David A. and Daniel W. Martin
    1973   Report of the Dolores River Project archaeological
                reconnaissance 1972-1973. Midwest Archaeological
                Center, National Park Service, Lincoln. xeroxed.

Breternitz, David A. and Cory D. Breternitz
    1973   Inventory of cliff dwellings, Johnson Canyon drainage,
                Ute Mountain Indian Reservation, 1972. Bureau of
                Indian Affairs, Albuouerque. xeroxed.

    1975   Cultural resources recorded for the BLM - 75 Montelores
                Project. Bureau of Land Management, Montrose. xeroxed.

Breternitz, David A., Larry V. Nordby, and Paul R. Nickens
    1974   Activities of the University of Colorado Mesa Verde
                Archaeological Research Center for 1974. Southwestern
                Lore 40:15-22.

Breternitz, David A., Arthur H. Rohn, and Elizabeth A. Morris
    1974   Prehistoric ceramics of the Mesa Verde Region. Museum
                of Northern Arizona, Ceramic Series 5.

Breternitz, David A. and Adrian S. White
    1976   Emergency stabilization of 5MT264 East Rock Canyon,
                Colorado. Bureau of Land Management, Montrose. xeroxed.

Breternitz, David A. and Paul R. Williams
    1976   Cultural resources recorded for the BLM - Fall 75
                Montrose Project. Bureau of Land Management, Montrose.
                xeroxed.

Brew, John O.
    1946   The archaeology of Alkali Ridge, southeastern Utah.
                Papers of the Peabody Museum of Archaeology and
                Ethnology 2:1-345.

Brisbin, Joel M.
    n.d.   Description of site 5MT228. Individual site report.
                Office of the State Archaeologist, Denver. xeroxed.

Brisbin, Joel M. and Charlotte J. Brisbin
    n.d.   Contributions to the sites being excavated in the
                north McElmo drainage area of southwestern Colorado
                (Ida Jean site). Ft. Lewis College, Durango. xeroxed.

    n.d.   Contributions to the sites being excavated in the
                north McElmo drainage area of southwestern Colorado
                (Sheme site). Ft. Lewis College, Durango. xeroxed.

Brooks, Danny
    1974   Prehistoric soil and water control in the American
                  Southwest: a case study. Unpublished M.A. thesis.
                  Department of Anthropology, Northern Arizona University,
                  Flagstaff.

Brown, Joy
    1975   Preliminary report on the 1975 excavations at site
                  5MT3 near Yellowjacket, Colorado. Southwestern Lore
                  41(4):47-50.

    n.d.   The environmental setting of the Yellowjacket sites and
                  a brief history of previous archaeological investigations
                  in the area. Department of Anthropology, University
                  of Colorado, Boulder. xeroxed.

Bryan, Kirk
    1925   Date of channel trenching (arroyo cutting) in the arid
                  Southwest. Science 62(1607):338-344.

Buge, David E. and James Schoenwetter
    1971   Pollen studies at Chimney Rock Mesa, Colorado. U.S.
                  Forest Service, San Juan National Forest, Durango.
                  xeroxed.

    1977   Pollen studies at Chimney Rock Mesa. In Archaeological
                  investigations at Chimney Rock Mesa 1970-1972, by Frank
                  W. Eddy. Colorado Archaeological Society, Memoir 1:77-80.

Bullene, Emma
    1905   The psychic history of the Cliff Dwellers. Reed
                  Publishing Co., Denver.

Bureau of Indian Affairs, Ignacio
    1965   Soil and range inventory of the Ute Mountain Indian
                  Reservation, Colorado and New Mexico. Branch of
                  Land Operations, Phoenix Area Office. xeroxed.

    1966   Soil and range inventory, Southern Ute Reservation,
                  Colorado. Branch of Roads, Phoenix Area Office.
                  xeroxed.

    1968   Cliff Dwellers survey, Lister Project. Ute Mountain
                  Indian Reservation. xeroxed.

Burgh, Richard
    1933   Cliff Dweller burial customs. Mesa Verde Notes 4:5-7.

Burgh, Robert F.

 1932a Archaeological methods. <u>Mesa Verde Notes</u> 3(13).

 1932b Diseases among prehistoric Pueblo peoples. <u>Mesa Verde Notes</u> 3(2).

 1934 The Far View group of ruins. <u>Mesa Verde Notes</u> 5:32-36.

 1937 Mesa Verde coiled basketry. <u>Mesa Verde Notes</u> 7(2):7.

 1949 Archaeological fieldwork of the University of Colorado Museum in 1947. Paper presented at the 1949 Plains Conference.

Butman, C. H.

 1916 The Sun Temple in Mesa Verde Park; a lesson in ancient American history. <u>Scientific American Supplement</u> 81: 312-313.

Camilli, Eileen

 1976 Environmental constraint at Hovenweep, 1974 sites. In Hovenweep 1975, by Joseph C. Winter. <u>San Jose State University Archeological Report</u>, No. 2:197-214.

Camilli, Eileen and J. C. Winter

 1975 Plant distribution, environmental constraint and farm site location at Hovenweep. In Hovenweep 1974, by Joseph C. Winter. <u>San Jose State University Archaeological Report</u>, No. 1:Appendix.

Carlson, Roy L.

 1963 Basketmaker III sites near Durango, Colorado. <u>University of Colorado Studies</u>, <u>Series in Anthropology</u>, No. 8.

Carpenter, Scott L.

 1975 Archaeological investigation of selected BLM lands in the Sand Canyon vicinity. Bureau of Land Management, Montrose. xeroxed.

Casey, T. Allen

 1937 Rheumatic Cliff Dwellers. <u>Mesa Verde Notes</u> 7(2):1-4.

Cassidy, Francis

 1965 Fire Temple, Mesa Verde National Park. In The great kivas of Chaco Canyon and their relationships, by Gordon Vivian and Paul Reiter. <u>School of American Research</u>, <u>Moncgraph</u> 22:73-81.

Cattanath, George S., Jr.
    1972   Wetherill Mesa excavations, Long House, Mesa Verde
                National Park, 2 Vols. Wetherill Project, Contribution
                51. National Park Service.

Caywood, L. R.
    1934   Mesa Verde sandals. Mesa Verde Notes 5:19-23.

Ceram, C. W.
    1972   The first American, a story of North American archaeology.
                New American Library, New York.

Chapin, F. H.
    1890   Cliff dwellings of the Mancos Canyons. American
                Antiquarian 12:193-210.

    1892   The land of the Cliff Dwellers. W. B. Clarke, Boston.

Chapman, A.
    1916   Among the ruins of Mesa Verde. Out West 44:153-160.
                Colorado Springs.

    1917   Among the cliff ruins of Mesa Verde National Park.
                Normal Instructor and Primary Plans (March). Danville,
                New York.

    1925   The story of Colorado, New York.

Clarke, Steven K.
    1974   A method for the estimation of prehistoric Pueblo
                populations. Kiva 39:283-287.

Cline, Pratt
    1935a   The seed of seeds. Mesa Verde Notes 6(2):14.

    1935b   Some place names of Mesa Verde. Mesa Verde Notes
                6:11-13.

Cockayne, Caroline
    1976   Ground stone tools. In Hovenweep 1975, by Joseph C.
                Winter. San Jose State University Archeological
                Report, No. 2:62-69.

Collins, Susan
    1970   Pottery distribution, Wetherill Mesa salvage: summer
                1970. Department of Anthropology, University of Colorado,
                Boulder. xeroxed.

Colyer, M.
    n.d. a   Macroscopic constituents of human and bear feces,
             Step House. Mesa Verde National Park, Colorado.
             xeroxed.

    n.d. b   Untitled list of coprolite components from Mug House
             feces. Mesa Verde National Park, Colorado. xeroxed.

    n.d. c   Untitled list of coprolite constituents from Long House
             feces. Mesa Verde National Park, Colorado. xeroxed.

Colyer, M. and D. Osbourne
    1965   Screening soil and fecal samples for recovery of small
             specimens. In Contributions of the Wetherill Mesa
             Archaeological Project, edited by D. Osbourne. Society
             for American Archaeology, Memoir 31(2):186-192.

Contract 14-11-0008-0590-27
    1966   Progress report upon inventory of archaeological
             remains on land controlled by BLM in Cortez-Dove Creek
             area of southwestern Colorado. Department of Anthropology,
             University of Colorado, Boulder. xeroxed.

Corbyn, Ronald C.
    1969   A study of the Mesa Verde stone age collection. Mesa
             Verde National Park, Colorado. xeroxed.

Cordell, Linda S.
    1972   Settlement pattern changes at Wetherill Mesa, Colorado:
             a test case for computer simulation in archaeology.
             Unpublished Ph. D. dissertation. Department of
             Anthropology, University of California, Santa Barbara.

    1975   Predicting site abandonment at Wetherill Mesa. Kiva
             40(3):189-202.

Cornelius, Olive Frasier
    1935   Basketmaker sandals? Southwestern Lore 3(4):74-78.

Cornelius, Temple H.
    1941   Footwear worn in San Juan basin in prehistoric times.
             Sherds and Points 2(8). San Juan Chapter, Colorado
             Archaeological Society, Durango.

Cowan, J. L.
    1910   Prehistoric apartment houses of the Southwest. Overland
             Monthly (2nd series) 44:340-346. San Francisco.

Cross, Whitman and Esper S. Larson
    1935   A brief review of the geology of the San Juan region
                of southwestern Colorado. <u>U.S. Geological Survey</u>,
                <u>Bulletin</u> 893.

Crotensburg, C. N.
    1900   Cliff Dwellers ruins. <u>American Antiquarian</u> 22:400-401.

Culligan, Colleen M.
    1976   Functional typology of the Hovenweep stone tool assemblage.
                In Hovenweep 1975, by Joseph C. Winter. <u>San Jose State</u>
                <u>University Archeological Report</u>, <u>No.</u> 2:51-61.

Cummings, Byron
    1910   The ancient inhabitants of the San Juan valley.
                <u>Bulletin, University of Utah, 2nd Archaeological Number</u>,
                3(2):part 2.

    1935   The archaeology of the Southwest. <u>Kiva</u> 1(1).

    1938   Kivas of the San Juan drainage. <u>Kiva</u> 3(7 and 8):25-30.

    1953   <u>First inhabitants of Arizona and the Southwest</u>. Cummings
                Publication Council, Tucson.

Current, William and Vincent Scully
    1971   <u>Pueblo architecture of the Southwest</u>. University of
                Texas Press, Austin.

Cutler, Hugh C. and Winton Meyer
    1965   Corn and cucurbits from Wetherill Mesa. In Contri-
                butions of the Wetherill Mesa Archaeological Project,
                assembled by Douglas Osbourne. <u>Society for American</u>
                <u>Archaeology</u>, <u>Memoir</u> 19:136-152.

Daniels, Helen Sloan
    1936   Durango Public Library Museum Project of the
                Archaeological Department, National Youth Administration
                1 (parts 1 and 2). Durango Public Library.

    1937   Durango Public Library Museum Project, National Youth
                Administration 2. Durango Public Library.

    1938a   Durango Public Library Museum Project, National Youth
                Administration 3:33. Durango Public Library.

    1938b   Carnegie Institute gets federal permits for Durango
                area (editorial, chapter and field notes). <u>Southwestern</u>
                <u>Lore</u> 4(1).

1940a Report of the Durango Public Library Museum Project of the National Youth Administration, La Plata County, Colorado. Durango Public Library. mimeographed.

1940b Basketmakers chipped axe. Sherds and Points 2. San Juan Chapter, Colorado Archaeological Society, Durango.

1940c Durango's contribution to Southwestern archaeology. Sherds and Points 12. San Juan Chapter, Colorado Archaeological Society, Durango.

1940d Excavation in Griffith Heights. Sherds and Points 5. San Juan Chapter, Colorado Archaeological Society, Durango.

1940e Summary of National Youth Administration excavation at Griffith Heights. Museum Project of the National Youth Administration 3:24-28. Durango Public Library.

1940f Valley home at Falls Creek. Sherds and Points 8. San Juan Chapter, Colorado Archaeological Society, Durango.

1954 Pictographs. In Basketmaker II sites near Durango, Colorado, by E. H. Morris and Robert F. Burgh. Carnegie Institute of Washington, Publication 604:87-88.

Daniels, M.
1916a Mesa Verde and Casa Grande National Parks. American Forestry 22:139-145.

1916b Ancient cliff dwellings of the Mesa Verde. American Institute of Architects Journal 4:384-88. Washington, D. C.

Davis, Emmalou
1965 Small pressures and cultural drift as explanations for abandonment of the San Juan area, New Mexico and Arizona. American Antiquity 30:353-355.

Dean, Jeffrey S.
1975 Tree ring dates from Colorado W: Durango area. Laboratory of Tree Ring Research, Tucson.

Dean, Jeffrey S. and William J. Robinson
1976 Dendroclimatic variability in the American Southwest A.D. 680 to 1970. Laboratory of Tree Ring Research, Tucson.

16

Dean, Nowland K.
1961   Fishes taken on the Navajo Expedition, 1960. In Ecological studies of the flora and fauna of Navajo Reservoir Basin, Colorado and New Mexico, edited by Angus M. Woodbury. University of Utah Anthropological Papers, No. 55:119-122.

Dean, Nowland K. and A. Dean Stock
1961   Amphibians and reptiles of the Navajo Reservoir Basin. In Ecological studies of the flora and fauna of Navajo Reservoir Basin, Colorado and New Mexico, edited by Angus M. Woodbury. University of Utah Anthropological Papers, No. 55:123-127.

DeBloois, Evan, Dee Green, and Henry Wylie
1974   A test of the impact of pinyon-juniper chaining on archaeological sites. Archeological Reports, Intermountain Region. U.S. Forest Service, Ogden, Utah.

Del Pero, Gail
1976   Computer seriation of Hovenweep ceramics. In Hovenweep 1975, by Joseph C. Winter. San Jose State University Archaeological Report, No. 2:36-43.

1977   Sampling procedures, 1974-1975: physiographic analysis of Hovenweep survey quadrants. In Hovenweep 1976, by Joseph C. Winter. San José State University Archeological Report, No. 3:159-169.

Dennison, James
1933   Scratches under the surface of the Mesa Verde. Mesa Verde Notes 4(2):12-13.

Dick, Herbert
1951   The present status of Colorado archaeology (abstract). Journal of the Colorado-Wyomirg Academy of Science 4:23.

1952   Symposium on Colorado archaeology: southwestern Colorado (abstract). Journal of the Colorado-Wyoming Academy of Science 4:26.

1953   The status of Colorado archaeology with a bibliographic guide. Southwestern Lore 28(4):53-77.

Dittert, Alfred E., Jr.
1963   Orientation of the highway and railroad salvage excavations. In Pueblo period sites in the Piedra River Section, Navajo Reservoir District, assembled by Alfred E. Dittert, Jr., and Frank W. Eddy. Museum of New Mexico Papers in Anthropology, No. 10:9-12.

Dittert, Alfred E., Jr., Jim J. Hester and Frank W. Eddy
    1961   An archaeological survey of the Navajo Reservoir District, northwestern New Mexico. Monographs of the School of American Research and the Museum of New Mexico, No. 23.

Dittert, Alfred E. and Frank W. Eddy
    1963   Pueblo period sites in the Piedra Section, Navajo Reservoir District. Museum of New Mexico Papers in Anthropology, No. 10.

Dobra, Lorraine
    n.d.   Paleo-ethnobotanical remains from 5LP110 and 5LP111. In The Durango South Project: archaeological salvage of two late Basketmaker III sites in the Durango District, by John D. Gooding. Colorado Archaeological Society, Memoir (In press, ms. 1977).

Dominguez, F. A. and S. O. deEscalante
    1854   Diario y derroto de los RR. PP. Fr. Francisco Anastasio
    (1777)   Domingues y Fr. Silvestre Velez de Escalante para descubirel camino desde el Presidio de Santa Fe del Nueva Mexico, al de Monterey, en la California Septentional. Documentos para la Historia de Mexico, 2 d ser, 1:338-339. Mexico.

Donance, E. and J. Donance
    1920   The Mesa Verde Park and its prehistoric ruins. Munsey's Magazine 61:90-98. New York.

Dondelinger, N. W.
    1944   Stone images in southern Colorado. American Antiquity 10:59-64.

Douglas, A. E.
    1938   Southwestern dated ruins. Tree Ring Bulletin 5:10-13.

    1940   Compression wood and the recent chronology in Mesa Verde firs. Tree Ring Bulletin 6(3):23-24.

    1949   Note on the early Durango collections. Tree Ring Bulletin 15(4).

Douglas, Charles L.
    1965   Biological techniques in archaeology. In Contributions of the Wetherill Mesa Archaeological Project, assembled by D. Osbourne. Society for American Archaeology, Memoir 19.

Dozier, Edward P.
    1965   Southwestern social units and archaeology. _American_
                Antiquity 31:38-47.

Dubois, Coert
    1905   The Mesa Verde National Park. _58th U.S. Congress 3rd_
                Session, _House Report 3703_, (Ser. No. 4761). Washington,
                D. C.

Durango Herald
    1889   Catalogue of ancient Aztec relics from the Mancos
                Canyon, La Plata County, southwestern Colorado.
                Colorado State Historical Museum, Denver. xeroxed.

Durrant, Stephen D. and Nowland K. Dean
    1961   Mammals of Navajo Reservoir Basin in Colorado and
                New Mexico. In Ecological studies of the flora and
                fauna of Navajo Reservoir Basin, Colorado and New
                Mexico, edited by Angus M. Woodbury. _University of_
                Utah Anthropological Papers, _No._ 55:155-182.

Eddy Frank W.
    1961   Excavations at Los Pinos Phase sites in the Navajo
                Reservoir District. _Museum of New Mexico Papers in_
                Anthropology, _No._ 4.

    1963a   Cultural considerations in the study of prehistoric
                animals. In Vertebrate remains and past environmental
                reconstruction in the Navajo Reservoir District, by
                A. H. Harris. _Museum of New Mexico Papers in Anthro-_
                pology, _No._ 11.

    1963b   Excavations at the Candelaria site, LA4406. In Pueblo
                period sites in the Piedra River Section, Navajo
                Reservoir District, assembled by Alfred E. Dittert,
                Jr., and Frank W. Eddy. _Museum of New Mexico Papers_
                in Anthropology, _No._ 10:13-43.

    1966   Prehistory in the Navajo Reservoir District, north-
                western New Mexico. _Museum of New Mexico Papers in_
                Anthropology, _No._ 15(parts 1 and 2).

    1968   Culture ecology and the prehistory of the Navajo
                Reservoir District. Unpublished Ph. D. dissertation.
                Department of Anthropology, University of Colorado,
                Boulder.

    1972a   Cultural ecology and the prehistory of the Navajo
                Reservoir District. _Southwestern Lore_ 38(1 and 2):1-73.

1972b   Archaeological report covering the Chimney Rock. Site survey and excavations at the Chimney Rock Pueblo 5AA83. U.S. Forest Service, San Juan National Forest, Durango. xeroxed.

1973a   Pueblo adaptions in the Upper San Juan basin of New Mexico and Colorado, A. D. 1-1125. Department of Anthropology, University of Colorado, Boulder. xeroxed.

1973b   Final archaeological report covering research at the Chimney Rock Mesa 1970-1972. U.S. Forest Service, San Juan National Forest, Durango. xeroxed.

1974   Population dislocation in the Navajo Reservoir District, New Mexico and Colorado. American Antiquity 39:75-84.

1975   A settlement model for reconstructing prehistoric social organization at Chimney Rock Mesa, southern Colorado. In Collected papers in honor of Florence Hawley Ellis, edited by Theodor Frisbie. Papers of the Archaeological Society of New Mexico 2.

1977   Archaeological investigations at Chimney Rock Mesa: 1970-1972. Colorado Archaeological Society, Memoir 1.

Eddy, Frank W. and Harold E. Degne
1964   Soil tests on alluvial and archeological deposits, Navajo Reservoir District. El Palacio 71(4):5-21.

Eklren, C. B. and F. N. Houser
1958   Stratigraphy and structure of the Ute Mountains, Montezuma County, Colorado. In Guidebook to the geology of Paradox Basin, edited by Albert F. Sanborn, pp. 74-75. International Association of Petroleum Geology, Salt Lake City.

Elisha, M. J.
1968   The present status of Basketmaker II and III sites in Colorado. Southwestern Lore 34(2):33-46.

Ellis, Florence Hawley
1936   Field manual of prehistoric Southwestern pottery types. University of New Mexico Bulletin 291.

Ellwood, Priscilla B.
1973   MT-1, a Basketmaker III site near Yellow Jacket, Colorado - ceramic analysis. University of Colorado Museum, Boulder. xeroxed.

1974   Analysis of whole ceramic vessels of MT-1 Porter Pueblo,
     Yellow Jacket, Colorado. University of Colorado Museum,
     Boulder. xeroxed.

n.d.   Ceramics of Durango South. In The Durango South Project:
     archaeological salvage of two late Basketmaker III sites
     in the Durango District, by John D. Gooding. Colorado
     Archaeological Society, Memoir (In press, ms. 1977).

Emslie, Steven D.
 1975   Petrographic analysis of Mesa Verde lithics. Journal
     of the Colorado-Wyoming Academy of Science 7:2.

 1977a Interpretation of faunal remains from archaeological
     sites in Mancos Canyon, southwestern Colorado. Unpublished
     M.A. thesis. Department of Anthropology, University of
     Colorado, Boulder.

 1977b Excavations at site 5MTUMR2785, Mancos Canyon, Ute
     Mountain Ute Homelands, Colorado. Department of
     Anthropology, University of Colorado, Boulder. xeroxed.

 n.d.   Shape analysis of ceramics from three Mesa Verde sites.
     Department of Anthropology, University of Colorado,
     Boulder. xeroxed.

Erdman, James A.
 1962   Ecology of the pinyon-juniper woodland of Wetherill
     Mesa, Mesa Verde National Park, Colorado. Unpublished
     M.A. thesis. University of Colorado, Boulder.

 1970   Pinyon-juniper succession after natural fires on
     residual soils of Mesa Verde, Colorado. Brigham Young
     University Science Bulletin, Biological Series 11(2).

Erdman, James A., Charles L. Douglas and John W. Marr
 1969   Environment of Mesa Verde Colorado. National Park
     Service Archaeological Research Series, 7-B.

Euler, Robert C.
 1963   A dedication to the memory of Edgar Lee Hewett, 1865-
     1946. Arizona and the West 5(4):186-190.

Fala, F. J.
 1939   Fire! Fire! Fire! Mesa Verde Notes 9(1).

Farmer, T. Reid
 1975   A factor analysis of some ceramics from Mancos Canyon,
     Colorado. Department of Anthropology, University of
     Colorado, Boulder. xeroxed.

1977   Salvage archaeology in Mancos Canyon, Colorado, 1975. Unpublished M.A. thesis. Department of Anthropology, University of Colorado, Boulder.

Farmer, T. Reid and Steven D. Emslie
1976   Archaeological inventory of proposed right of way, Johnson Canyon to Lion House overlook. Bureau of Indian Affairs, Albuquerque. xeroxed.

Fenega, Franklin
1956   Excavations at the Ignacio, Colorado, field camp site LA2605. In Pipeline archaeology, reports of Salvage Operations in the Southwest on El Paso Natural Gas Company Project 1950 #53, edited by Fred Wendorf, pp. 207-214. Laboratory of Anthropology, Santa Fe.

Fetterman, Jerry E.
1977   Archaeological resources of the Southern Ute Indian Reservation, Colorado. Bureau of Indian Affairs, Ignacio. xeroxed.

Fewkes, Jesse Walter
1896   A contribution to ethnobotany. American Anthropologist 9:14-21.

1904   Two summer's work in Pueblo ruins. Bureau of American Ethnology, 22nd Annual Report (part 1):3-195.

1908a   Mesa Verde, Colorado, field notes. Jesse Walter Fewkes papers. Smithsonian Institution. xeroxed.

1908b   Report on excavation and repair of the Spruce Tree House in May and June 1908. United States Department of Interior, First Annual Report:490-505.

1908c   Ventilators in ceremonial rooms of prehistoric cliff dwellings. American Anthropologist 10:387-398.

1909a   Antiquities of the Mesa Verde National Park, Spruce-Tree House. Bureau of American Ethnology, Bulletin 41.

1909b   The preservation of cliff-dwellings. Science 30:(779).

1910a   Cremation in cliff dwellings. Records of the Past 9:54-56.

1910b   Note on the occurrence of adobes in cliff dwellings. American Anthropologist 12:434-436.

1910c   The excavation and repair of Cliff Palace, Mesa Verde National Park, Colorado. Department of the Interior, Report for 1909 (1):483-503.

1911   Antiquities of the Mesa Verde National Park, Cliff
Palace. Bureau of American Ethnology, Bulletin 51.

1916a   A prehistoric Mesa Verde pueblo and its people (Far
View House). Smithsonian Institution, Annual Report:
461-488.

1916b   Excavation and repair of Sun Temple, Mesa Verde National
Park. National Park Service, Washington.

1916c   Excavations in the Mesa Verde Park. Old Santa Fe
3:161-165.

1916d   Prehistoric remains in New Mexico, Colorado, and Utah.
In Smithsonian Miscellaneous Collections 66(17):76-92.

1916e   The cliff ruins in Fewkes Canyon, Mesa Verde National
Park, United States Department of Interior, National
Park Service. In Holmes Anniversary Volume, pp. 96-117.
Smithsonian Institution, Washington, D. C.

1916f   The relation of Sun Temple, a new type of ruin lately
excavated in the Mesa Verde National Park, to prehistoric "towers." Washington Academy of Sciences
Journal 6:212-221. Washington, D. C.

1917a   Far View House - a pure type of Pueblo ruin. Art and
Archaeology 6:133-141. Baltimore and Washington, D. C.

1917b   Archaeological investigations in New Mexico, Colorado,
and Utah. Smithsonian Miscellaneous Collections
68(1):1-38.

1917c   Prehistoric remains in New Mexico, Colorado and Utah.
Smithsonian Miscellaneous Collections 66(17):76-92.

1917d   Ruins in vicinity of Dolores, Colorado: Ruin Canyon,
McClean Basin. Jesse Walter Fewkes papers. Smithsonian
Institution. xeroxed.

1917e   The first Pueblo ruin in Colorado. Mentioned in Spanish
documents. Science 46(1185):255-256.

1917f   The Mesa Verde types of pueblos. Proceedings of the
National Academy of Sciences 3:497-501.

1918a   Castles and towers of the Hovenweep. Railroad Red
Book 35:11-14. Denver.

1918b   Field notes for Dolores Colorado and Mesa Verde. Jesse Walter Fewkes papers. Smithsonian Institution. xeroxed.

1918c   Prehistoric ruins in southwestern Colorado and southeastern Utah. Smithsonian Miscellaneous Collections 68(12):108-133.

1918d   Prehistoric towers and castles of the Southwest. Art and Archaeology 7:353-366. Baltimore and Washington, D. C.

1919a   Prehistoric villages, castles and towers of southwestern Colorado. Bureau of American Ethnology, Bulletin 70.

1919b   A unique form of prehistoric pottery. Scientific American Supplement 87:377, 384.

1919c   Two types of Southwestern cliff houses. In Smithsonian Institution, Annual Report:421-427.

1920a   Ancient remains in Colorado; the Mesa Verde National Park, landmark of a lost race. Scientific American 122:598, 606, 608- 610.

1920b   Architectural types of Mesa Verde. Smithsonian Institution Annual Report:58-61.

1920c   Field work on the Mesa Verde National Park, Colorado, 1919. In Explorations and field work of the Smithsonian Institution in 1919. Smithsonian Miscellaneous Collections 70(2):68-80.

1920d   Field work on the Mesa Verde National Park, Colorado. Smithsonian Miscellaneous Collections 72(1):47-64.

1920e   Fire worship of the Hopi Indians. Smithsonian Institution Annual Report:159-610.

1920f   New fire house, a ruin lately excavated in the Mesa Verde. Art and Archaeology 10:44-46. Baltimore and Washington, D. C.

1920g   Preserving aboriginal architecture, masterpieces to posterity. World 34:247-248. Boston.

1920h   Square Tower House. Southern Workman 49:309-314. Hampton, Virginia.

1920i   The genesis of the cliff dwellings. Washington
         Academy of Sciences Journal 10:334-335. Washington,
         D. C.

1921a   Excavating cliff dwellings in Mesa Verde. Scientific
         American 3:9-13.

1921b   Field work on the Mesa Verde National Park. Smithsonian
         Miscellaneous Collections 72:75-79.

1921c   Two types of Southwestern cliff houses. Smithsonian
         Institution Annual Report:421-426.

1922a   A prehistoric observatory. Literary Digest 75:27.
         New York.

1923   The Hovenweep National Monument. American Anthropolo-
         gist 25(2):145-155.

1925a   The Hovenweep National Monument. Smithsonian Insti-
         tution Annual Report:465-480.

1925b   Archaeological field work on the Mesa Verde National
         Park, Colorado. Smithsonian Miscellaneous Collections
         74:89-115.

1926   The chronology of Mesa Verde. American Journal of
         Archaeology (2nd Series) 30:270-282. Concord, New
         Hampshire.

Fewkes, J. W. and J. A. Jeancon
    1921   Field work on the Mesa Verde National Park. Smithsonian
             Miscellaneous Collections 72(6).

Fletcher, Maurice S. (Editor)
    1976   The Wetherills of Mesa Verde: autobiography of
             Benjamin Alfred Wetherill. Associated University
             Presses, Cranbury, N. J.

Flora, I. F.
    1940a   Mesa Verde and Mesa Verde's pithouses. Sherds and
             Points 3. San Juan Chapter, Colorado Archaeological
             Society, Durango.

    1940b   A Durango home in 630 A.D. Sherds and Points 4.
             San Juan Chapter, Colorado Archaeological Society,
             Durango.

    1940c   The work of a pot hunter. Sherds and Points 6. San
             Juan Chapter, Colorado Archaeological Society, Durango.

1940d   Hillside home at Falls Creek. Sherds and Points 7.
San Juan Chapter, Colorado Archaeological Society,
Durango.

1940e   Durango resident of 500 B.C. Sherds and Points 9.
San Juan Chapter, Colorado Archaeological Society,
Durango.

1940f   Culture and pottery vessel. Sherds and Points 10.
San Juan Chapter, Colorado Archaeological Society,
Durango.

1940g   Original tabloid editor, 603 A.D. Sherds and Points
11. San Juan Chapter, Colorado Archaeological Society,
Durango.

1940h   The smokeless stove of the aborigines. Sherds and
Points 13. San Juan Chapter, Colorado Archaeological
Society, Durango.

1940i   Obtaining weather records of the Past. Sherds and
Points 14. San Juan Chapter, Colorado Archaeological
Society, Durango.

1941a   Archaeological story of Durango Colorado by local
amateurs. Sherds and Points 12 (article 567). San
Juan Chapter, Colorado Archaeological Society, Durango.

1941b   Esther, a Durango citizen of 500 B.C. Sherds and
Points 2(1). San Juan Chapter, Colorado Archaeological
Society, Durango.

1941c   Descendants of the Folsom point. Sherds and Points
2(2). San Juan Chapter, Colorado Archaeological
Society, Durango.

1941d   Durango Man of 800 B.C. Sherds and Points 2(5). San
Juan Chapter, Colorado Archaeological Society, Durango.

1941e   Modern Man in a prehistoric bedroom. Sherds and Points
2(6). San Juan Chapter, Colorado Archaeological Society,
Durango.

1941f   Whats a prehistoric what's it? Sherds and Points 2(7).
San Juan Chapter, Colorado Archaeological Society,
Durango.

1941g   Prehistoric ammunition. Can you reload them? Sherds
and Points 2(9). San Juan Chapter, Colorado Archaeological
Society, Durango.

1941h   Basketmaker III makes an axe (or hoe). Sherds and Points
           2(11). San Juan Chapter, Colorado Archaeological Society,
           Durango.

1941i   These hieroglyphics defy translation. Sherds and Points
           2(12). San Juan Chapter, Colorado Archaeological Society,
           Durango.

1941j   Type pottery of the BM III aborigines. Sherds and
           Points 2(13). San Juan Chapter, Colorado Archaeological
           Society, Durango.

1941k   Durango merchandise 620 A.D. Sherds and Points 2(14).
           San Juan Chapter, Colorado Archaeological Society,
           Durango.

1941l   The ground axe (or hoe) of the aborigines. Sherds and
           Points 2(16). San Juan Chapter, Colorado Archaeological
           Society, Durango.

1959   The story of Esther and her kin. Mesa Verde National
           Park, Colorado. xeroxed.

n.d.   Contrast chart revised from 1938 preliminary survey of
           prehistoric cultures of the Durango Colorado district.
           Manuscript #1981, C.T. Hurst Collection. Western
           State College, Gunnison.

Flora, I. F. and H. S. Daniels
    1940   Sherds and points, Durango amateur archaeological story.
               (Collection of reprinted newspaper articles bound in
               one volume). Durango Public Library.

Folsom-Dickerson, W. E. S.
    1968   Cliff dwellers. DeNaylor Company, New York.

Franke, Paul R.
    1932a   Incised pottery designs on building blocks of Mesa
               Verde masonry. Mesa Verde Notes 3:29-32.

    1932b   The Mesa Verde. Nature Magazine 19:289-291, 329.

    1932c   Museum acquisitions for 1932. Mesa Verde Notes 3:1-5.

    1933a   Museum acquisitions for 1933. Mesa Verde Notes 4(1):1-2.

    1933b   New dates for Mesa Verde ruins. Mesa Verde Notes
               4(1):19-20.

    1934a   A unique pot from Mesa Verde. Mesa Verde Notes 5(2).

1934b   Sun symbol markings. <u>Mesa Verde Notes</u> 5:7-12.

1935a   Bibliography for Mesa Verde National Park. <u>Mesa Verde National Park - Occasional Papers</u> 1.

1935b   Mesa Verde's place in the Southwest story. <u>Southwestern Lore</u> 1:11-16.

Franke, Paul R. and Don Watson
    1936   An experimental corn field in Mesa Verde National Park. In Symposium on prehistoric agriculture, edited by D. O. Brand. <u>University of New Mexico Bulletin</u> 296, <u>Anthropological Series</u> 1(5):36-41.

Freeman, Ira S.
    1958   <u>A history of Montezuma County, Colorado</u>. Johnson Publishing Co., Boulder, Colorado.

Fritts, H. C., D. G. Smith and M. A. Stokes
    1965   The biological model for paleoclimatic interpretation of Mesa Verde tree-ring series. In Contributions of the Wetherill Mesa Archaeological Project, edited by D. Osbourne and B. S. Katz. <u>Society for American Archaeology, Memoir</u> 19:101-121.

Frowe, L. G.
    1906   The Mesa Verde National Park. <u>Modern World</u> 7(November). Baltimore.

Fuller, G.
    1910   Exploring the Mesa Verde. <u>Magazine of History</u> 11:33-39. New York.

Gannet, H.
    1880   Prehistoric ruins in southern Colorado. <u>Popular Science Monthly</u> 16:646-673

Gardner, J. H.
    1909   The coal field between Durango, Colorado and Manero, New Mexico. In Contributions to economic geology. <u>U.S. Geological Survey, Bulletin</u> 341:352-363.

Gelfand, Alaric M.
    1971   Bibliography on Southwestern Indian cultures. Bureau of Land Management, Montrose. xeroxed.

Getty, Harry T.
    1932   The tree rings, nature's timekeeper. <u>Mesa Verde Notes</u> 3:25-26.

1933   Pursuing the elusive tree ring. <u>Mesa Verde Notes</u> 4(2):14-16.

1935a   New dates from Mesa Verde. <u>Tree Ring Bulletin</u> 1(3):21-23.

1935b   New dates for Spruce Tree House, Mesa Verde. <u>Tree Ring Bulletin</u> 1(4):28-29.

1939   Report of dates from sites 1 and 2, southwestern Colorado. In Modified Basketmaker sites Ackmen Lowry area, southwestern Colorado, 1938 by Paul S. Martin and John Rinaldo. <u>Field Museum of Natural History Anthropological Series</u> 23(3):493-495.

Gillespie, William B.
    1975a   Preliminary report of excavations at the Ute Canyon site 5MTURM2347, Ute Mountain, Ute Homelands, Colorado. Bureau of Indian Affairs, Albuquerque. xeroxed.

    1975b   Multivariate analysis of ceramics from the Ute Canyon site, southwestern Colorado. Department of Anthropology, University of Colorado, Boulder. xeroxed.

    1975c   Toward a systematic model of prehistoric faunal exploitation in Mancos Canyon, southwestern Colorado. Department of Anthropology, University of Colorado, Boulder. xeroxed.

    1976   Culture change at the Ute Canyon site: a study of the pithouse-kiva transition in the Mesa Verde Region. Unpublished M.A. thesis. Department of Anthropology, University of Colorado, Boulder.

Gilmore, Frances and Louisa Wade Wetherill
    1934   <u>Traders to the Navahoes</u>. Houghton and Mifflin, New York.

Gilpin, L.
    1927   <u>Mesa Verde National Park. Reproductions from a series of photographs</u>. Colorado Springs.

    1941   <u>The Pueblos, a camera chronicle</u>. Hastings House, New York.

Goddard, P. E.
    1928   Deserted cities of the cliffs. <u>Magazine of History</u> 28:107-412.

    1931   Indians of the Southwest. <u>American Museum of Natural History Handbook Series</u>, No. 2.

Gooding, John D.
    1974   The highway salvage program in Colorado. <u>Southwestern</u>
                <u>Lore</u> 40(3 and 4):7-11.

    n.d.   The Durango South Project: archaeological salvage
                of two late Basketmaker III sites in the Durango
                District. <u>Colorado Archaeological Society</u>, <u>Memoir</u>
                (In press, ms. 1977).

Gooding, John D. and O. D. Hand
    n.d.   The site descriptions. In The Durango South Project:
                archaeological salvage of two late Basketmaker III
                sites in the Durango District, by John D. Gooding.
                <u>Colorado Archaeological Society</u>, <u>Memoir</u> (In press,
                ms. 1977).

Graham, Samuel A.
    1965   Entomology: an aid in archaeological studies. In
                Contributions of the Wetherill Mesa Archaeological
                Project, assembled by Douglas Osbourne. <u>Society for</u>
                <u>American Archaeology</u>, Memoir 19:167-174.

Green, C. H.
    n.d.   Catalogue of a unique collection of Cliff Dweller
    probably 1891 relics taken from the lately discovered ruins of
                southwestern Colorado and adjacent points of Utah,
                New Mexico, and Arizona. Mesa Verde National Park,
                Colorado. xeroxed.

Green, E. H.
    1954   Survey of the Pine River drainage area, southwestern
                Colorado, 1952-1954. <u>Southwestern Lore</u> 19(4):5-7.

Greene, Barbara and Marilyn K. Swift
    1976   Geology of 'Hovenweep in relation to possible lithic
                sources. In Hovenweep 1975, by Joseph C. Winter.
                <u>San Jose State University Archaeological Report</u>,
                <u>No.</u> 2:252-269.

Grimes, K. A.
    1923   Mesa Verde, land of ghosts dreams. <u>Normal Instructor</u>
                <u>and Primary Plans</u> 28:407-412. Dansville, New York.

Gunkel, L. W.
    1897   Ruins and picture writings in the canons of the McElmo
                and Hovenweep. <u>American Antiquarian</u> 9:223-226. Chicago.

Gumerman, G. J.
    1971   The distribution of prehistoric population aggregates.
                In Proceedings of the first annual meeting of the
                Southwestern Anthropological Research Group. <u>Prescott</u>
                <u>College Anthropological Reports</u>, <u>No.</u> 1.

Guthe, Alfred K.
    1949   Preliminary report on excavations in southwestern
                Colorado. American Antiquity 15(2):144-154.

Haas, William H.
    1916   Erosion features of the Mesa Verde. Illinois State
                Academy of Science, Transactions 19:211-219.

Hackett, C.
    1917   Mesa Verde: What does it mean? Railroad Red Book
                (January). Denver.

Hafen, L. R.
    1933   Colorado, the story of a Western commonwealth. Denver
                Peerless Publishing Co., Denver.

Hall, A. F.
    1938   Mesa Verde - a brief guide. Mesa Verde National Park,
                Colorado. xeroxed.

Hall, E. T.
    1944   Dendrochronological notes. In An archaeological study
                of Mancos Valley, southwestern Colorado and its position
                in the prehistory of the American Southwest, by Eric
                K. Reed, pp. 251-252. Unpublished Ph. D. thesis.
                Harvard University, Cambridge.

Hall, Hebert H. and Seville Flowers
    1961   Vascular plants found in the Navajo Reservoir Basin,
                1960, Colorado and New Mexico. In Ecological studies
                of the flora and fauna of Navajo Reservoir Basin,
                Colorado and New Mexico, edited by Angus M. Woodbury.
                University of Utah Anthropological Papers, No. 55:47-87.

Hallisey, Stephen J.
    1972a   A slablined firepit on Wetherill Mesa. Midwest
                Archaeological Center, National Park Service, Lincoln. .
                xeroxed.

    1972b   Site 1990, a Basketmaker III pithouse on Wetherill
                Mesa. Midwest Archaeological Center, National Park
                Service, Lincoln. xeroxed.

    1974   Salvage excavation of sites 5MTUMR2344 and 5MTUMR2347
                in Mancos Canyon, southwestern Colorado. Bureau of
                Indian Affairs, Albuquerque. xeroxed.

Hallisey, Steven J., Larry V. Nordby and David A. Breternitz
    1972   Wetherill Mesa salvage archaeology. National Park
                Service, Mesa Verde National Park, Colorado. xeroxed.

31

Haman, Jon
n.d.   Hovenweep National Monument survey sites. Hovenweep
            National Monument. xeroxed.

Hammett, Julia
1977   Analysis of 1976 ceramic collection. In Hovenweep
            1976, by Joseph C. Winter. San Jose State University
            Archaeological Report, No. 3:63-78.

Hand, O. D.
n.d.   Ground stone tools. In The Durango South Project:
            archaeological salvage of two late Basketmaker III
            sites in the Durango District, by John D. Gooding.
            Colorado Archaeological Society, Memoir (In press,
            ms. 1977).

Hardacre, G. C.
1878   The Cliff Dwellers. Science Monthly 17:266-276. London.

Harrill, Bruce G.
1976   Faunal remains from the Johnson Canyon cliff dwellings.
            In The Johnson-Lion Canyon Project: report of investi-
            gation III, assembled by Paul R. Nickens, pp. 65-97.
            Bureau of Indian Affairs, Albuquerque. xeroxed.

Harrill, Bruce G. and Cory D. Breternitz
1975   Dendrochronological analysis of the Johnson Canyon
            cliff dwellings. In The 1974 Johnson-Lion Canyon
            Project: report of investigation I, assembled by
            Paul R. Nickens, pp. 25-56. Bureau of Indian Affairs,
            Albuquerque. xeroxed.

1976   Chronology and cultural activity in Johnson Canyon
            cliff dwellings: interpretation from tree ring data.
            Journal of Field Archaeology 3(4):375-390.

Harrington, H. D.
1964   Manual of the plants of Colorado. Swallow Press, Inc.,
            Chicago.

Harris, Arthur H.
1963   Vertebrate remains and past environmental reconstruc-
            tion in the Navajo Reservoir District. Museum of New
            Mexico Papers in Anthropology, No. 11.

1971   The Chimney Rock area - modern ecology. U.S. Forest
            Service, San Juan National Forest, Durango, Colorado.
            xeroxed.

1977   Faunal remains from Chimney Rock Mesa. In Archaeological investigation at Chimney Rock Mesa: 1970-1972, by Frank W. Eddy. Colorado Archaeological Society, Memoir 1:73-76.

n.d.   The Chimney Rock area - modern ecology. Museum of Arid Land Biology, University of Texas, El Paso. xeroxed.

Harris, Arthur H. and F. W. Eddy
1963   Vertebrate remains and past environmental reconstruction in the Navajo Reservoir District. Museum of New Mexico Papers in Anthropology, No. 11.

Haury, Emil W.
1934   Climate and human history. Tree Ring Bulletin 1(2):13.

1938   Southwestern dated ruins II. Tree Ring Bulletin 4(3):3.

Haury, Emil W. and I. F. Flora
1937   Basketmaker III dates from the vicinity of Durango, Colorado. Tree Ring Bulletin 4(1):7-8.

Hayden, F. V.
1977   Biological and geographical atlas of Colorado and portions of adjacent territories, 1877. U.S. Geological and Geographical Surveys, Washington, D. C.

Hayes, Alden C.
1964   The archeological survey of Wetherill Mesa, Mesa Verde National Park - Colorado. National Park Service, Archaeological Research Series 7A.

1969   The Wetherill Mesa Project. Naturalist 20(2):18-25.

Hayes, A. C. and D. Osbourne
1961   Fixing site location with radio-direction finder at Mesa Verde. American Antiquity 27(1).

Hayes, Alden C. and James A. Lancaster
1962   Site 1060, a Basket Maker III pithouse on Chapin Mesa, Mesa Verde National Park. Tree Ring Bulletin 24(1-2): 14-16.

1968   Site 1060, a Basketmaker III pithouse on Chapin Mesa. In Contributions to Mesa Verde archaeology V, emergency archaeology in Mesa Verde National Park, Colorado, 1948-1966, edited by Robert H. Lister. University of Colorado Studies, Series in Anthropology, No. 15:65-68.

33

1975   Badger House Community, Mesa Verde National Park, Colorado. National Park Service Archaeological Research Series 7-E.

Henderson, J.
1927   The prehistoric peoples of Colorado. In Colorado: short studies of its past and present, pp. 1-22. Boulder.

Henderson, P.
1893   Cliff-dwellers houses. American Antiquarian 15:170-172. New York.

Herold, Joyce Lillian
1959   Prehistoric settlement and physical environment in the Mesa Verde area. Unpublished M.A. thesis. Department of Anthropology, University of Colorado, Boulder.

1961   Prehistoric settlement and physical environment in the Mesa Verde area. University of Utah Anthropological Papers, No. 53.

Hester, James J.
1962   Early Navajo migrations and acculturation in the Southwest. Museum of New Mexico Papers in Anthropology, No. 6.

1963   Excavations at the Serrano site LA4408. In Pueblo period sites in the Piedra River Section, Navajo Reservoir District, assembled by Alfred E. Dittert, Jr., and Frank W. Eddy. Museum of New Mexico Papers in Anthropology, No. 10:44-79.

1974   Archaeology in Colorado. Southwestern Lore 4(3 and 9): 1-5.

Hester, James J. and Joel L. Shiner
1963   Studies at Navajo period sites in the Navajo Reservoir District. Museum of New Mexico Papers in Anthropology, No. 9.

Hevley, Richard H.
1964   Pollen analysis of late Quaternary archaeological and Lacustrine sediments on the Colorado Plateau. Unpublished Ph. D. dissertation. University of Arizona, Tucson.

Hewett, Arthur F., Jr.
1968   The salvage excavation of site 1914, Navajo Hill. In Contributions to Mesa Verde archaeology V, emergency archaeology in Mesa Verde National Park, Colorado, 1943-1966, edited by Robert H. Lister. University of Colorado Studies, Series in Anthropology, No. 15.

Hewett, Edgar L.

1904a   Circular relating to historic and prehistoric ruins in
        the Southwest and their preservation. Government Printing
        Office, Washington.

1904b   A general view of the archaeology of the Pueblo region.
        Annual Report of the Smithsonian Institution:583-605.

1906-1909 Field notes. Bureau of Land Management, Montrose. xeroxed.

1920   Antiquities of Colorado. Art and Archaeology 10:39-43.
        Baltimore and Washington, D. C.

1930   Ancient life in the American Southwest. The Bobbs
        Merrill Co., Indianapolis, Indiana.

1943   Ancient life in the American Southwest. Tutor Publishing
        Co., New York.

Hibbets, Barry N.

1977a   An archaeological survey of the eight switch salvage
        timber sale, Dolores Ranger District. U.S. Forest
        Service, San Juan National Forest, Durango. xeroxed.

1977b   An archaeological survey of a proposed stock reservoir
        in the glade, Dolores Ranger District. U.S. Forest
        Service, San Juan National Forest, Durango. xeroxed.

1977c   An archaeological survey of a proposed stock reservoir
        on Stoner Mesa, Dolores Ranger District. U.S. Forest
        Service, San Juan National Forest, Durango. xeroxed.

1977d   An archaeological survey of the Corral Lake timber sale,
        Dolores Ranger District. U.S. Forest Service, San Juan
        National Forest, Durango. xeroxed.

Hicks, Patricia A.

1976   Projectile points: Hovenweep archeological surveys
        1974-1975. In Hovenweep 1975, by Joseph C. Winter.
        San Jose State University Archeological Report, No. 2:
        44-50.

1977   Projectile points, Hovenweep 1976. In Hovenweep 1976,
        by Joseph C. Winter. San Jose State University
        Archeological Report, No. 3:114-124.

Hodge, F. W.

1935   Boy scouts and pot-hunters. Masterkey 9:19-21.

Hoebel, E. Adamson
    1953   Underground kiva passages. American Antiquity 19:76.

Hoffman, E. L.
    1920   Why the Cliff Dwellers vanished. Scientific American
                123:630, 641, 642.

Holmes, W. H.
    1876   A notice of the ancient ruins of southwestern Colorado,
                examined during the summer of 1875. U.S. Geological
                and Geographic Survey, Bulletin 2:3-24.

    1878a   Cliff houses and ruins on the Mancos River. In Survey
                of the territories for 1876, edited by F. V. Hayden.
                U.S. Geological and Geographic Survey of the Territories,
                10th Annual Report:391-399.

    1878b   Report on the ancient ruins of southwestern Colorado,
                examined during the summers of 1875 and 1876. In Survey
                of the territories for 1876, edited by F. V. Hayden.
                U.S. Geological and Geographic Survey of the Territories,
                10th Annual Report:383-408.

    1886   Pottery of the ancient Pueblos. Bureau of American Ethnology,
                Fourth Annual Report:257-360.

    1919   Handbook of aboriginal American antiquities. Bureau of
                American Ethnology, Bulletin 60 (part 1).

    1920   Description of Yucca House. Art and Archaeology 10:42.
                Baltimore and Washington, D. C.

Holst, Michael
    1975   Faunal remains. In Hovenweep 1974, by Joseph C. Winter.
                San Jose State University Archaeological Report, No. 1:
                80-84.

Hornback, Anita
    1977   A study of lithic materials found in the 1976 field
                season of the Hovenweep Archeological Project. In
                Hovenweep 1976, by Joseph C. Winter. San Jose State
                University Archeological Report, No. 3:93-113.

Howard, Richard M.
    1969a   Discovery and establishment of Mesa Verde as a National
                Park. Naturalist 20(2):8-17.

    1969b   A most remarkable man--Gustaf Nordenskiold. Naturalist
                20(2):32-35.

1975   The Mesa Verde mug. American Indian Art 1(1):20-25.

Huntington, W. D.
   1953   Discovery of prehistoric ruins in Colorado 1854.
              Colorado Magazine 30(4):275-280.

Hurst, Blanche A.
   1957   A comparative study of the peripheral excavations of
              C. T. Hurst. Southwestern Lore 23(2):15-31.

Hurst, C. T.
   1944   Mesa Verde of Colorado. The Laurel 25(3).

   1946   Prehistoric Man in Colorado. The Brand Book. Denver
              Corral of the Westerners, Denver.

Hurst, C. T. and V. F. Lotrich
   1932   An unusual mug from Yellow Jacket Canyon. El Palacio
              33(21-22):195-198.

   1933   The Square Mug House of the Mesa Verde culture. Journal
              of the Colorado-Wyoming Academy of Science 1(5):70-71.

   1934   Another unusual bowl from Yellow Jacket Canyon. El
              Palacio 34(15-16):111-115.

   1935   An interesting Southwestern burial. Journal of the
              Colorado-Wyoming Academy of Science 2:63.

   1937   A Colorado burial of the proto-Mesa Verde culture.
              El Palacio 38(24, 25, 26):133-143.

Hutchinson, Daniel J. and Linda Knight
   1974   Cultural resource study - archaeological resource Oct.
              1972--Mar. 1974. Bureau of Land Management, Montrose.
              xeroxed.

Ingersoll, E.
   1883   Mesa Verde. In Knocking round the Rockies, pp. 162-172.
              New York.

   1928   Ruins in southwestern Colorado. Heye Foundation, Indian
              Notes 2:183-206. (Reprint of an article which first
              appeared in the New York Tribune, Nov. 3, 1874; it was
              the first published description of the ancient ruins of
              the Mesa Verde region.)

Ingmanson, J. Earl
   1969   The cultural sequence at the Mesa Verde. Naturalist
              20(2):1-12.

Iorns, W. V., C. H. Hembree, D. A. Phoenix, and G. L. Oakland
    1964   Water resources of the upper Colorado River basin:
              technical report. U.S. Geological Survey, Professional
              Paper 442.

Iorns, W. V., C. H. Hembree, and G. H. Oakland
    1965   Water resources of the upper Colorado River basin:
              technical report. U.S. Geological Survey, Professional
              Paper 441.

Irwin, James H.
    1966   Geology and availability of ground water on the Ute
              Mountain Indian Reservation, Colorado and New Mexico.
              U.S. Geological Survey, Water-Supply Paper 1576-G.

Irwin, W.
    1923   The land of the little people. Saturday Evening Post
              7:95-98.

Irwin-Williams, Cynthia
    1977   Black boxes and multiple working hypotheses: recon-
              structing the economy of early Southwest hunters.
              Kiva 42(3-4):285-299.

Ives, John C.
    1971a   Preliminary report of archaeological survey excavations
              by Fort Lewis College under permit #71-CO-021 on public
              lands under supervision of the Bureau of Land Management.
              Bureau of Land Management, Montrose. xeroxed.

    1971b   Preliminary report of archaeological excavations by
              Fort Lewis College under permit #70-CO-022 on public lands
              under supervision of the Bureau of Land Management 1970-71.
              Bureau of Land Management, Montrose. xeroxed.

    1972   Preliminary report of archaeological excavations by
              Fort Lewis College under permit #72-CO-022 and a survey
              under permit #70-CO-021 on public lands under supervision
              of the Bureau of Land Management 1972. Bureau of Land
              Management, Montrose. xeroxed.

    1976   Preliminary report of archaeological excavations by Fort
              Lewis College under permit #73-CO-034 on public lands
              under supervision of the Bureau of Land Management 1973.
              Bureau of Land Management, Montrose. xeroxed.

Jackson, W. H.
    1875   Ancient ruins in southwestern Colorado. U.S. Geological
              and Geographical Survey Bulletin (2nd series) 1:17-38.

1876a   Ancient ruins in southwestern Colorado. In U.S. Geological
         and Geographical Survey of the Territories, 8th Annual
         Report, by F. V. Hayden:368-381.

1876b   Ancient ruins in southwestern Colorado. American
         Naturalist 10(11):31-37, 161-165.

1878   Report on the ancient ruins examined in 1875 and 1877. In
         U.S. Geological and Geographical Survey of the Territories,
         10th Annual Report, by F. V. Hayden:411-429.

1924   First official visit to the cliff dwellings. Colorado
         Magazine 1(4):151-159.

1929   Discovery of the cliff ruins. In The pioneer photographer,
         pp. 226-242. Yonkers-on-Hudson, New York.

1940   Time exposure. The autobiography of William Henry
         Jackson. Putnam's Sons, New York.

Jeancon, J. A.
   1922a   Archaeological research in the northeastern San Juan
            basin of Colorado during the summer of 1921. The State
            Historical and Natural History Society of Colorado and
            the University of Denver, Denver.

   1922b   Two seasons work in Colorado. The State Historical and
            Natural History Society of Colorado - Bulletin. Denver.

   1924   Report on study and excavation of Stollsteimer Mesa,
            Colorado and Utah. Bureau of American Ethnology.
            Manuscript No. 1715. Washington, D. C.

   1925   Primitive Coloradoans. Colorado Magazine 2(1):35-40.

   1926   Pictographs of Colorado. Colorado Magazine 3(2):36-45.

   n.d.   Two ruin sites in Montezuma County, southwestern Colorado.
            Bureau of American Ethnology, Manuscript No. 3030.
            Washington, D. C.

Jeancon, J. A. and F. H. Douglas
   1930a   Periods of Pueblo culture and history. Denver Art
            Museum Leaflet 11.

   1930b   The Pueblo Golden Age. Denver Art Museum Leaflet 14.

Jeancon, J. A. and Frank H. H. Roberts, Jr.
   1923-24a Excavation work in the Pagosa-Piedra field during the
            season of 1922. Colorado Magazine 1(2, 3, 4):65-70,
            108-118, 163-173.

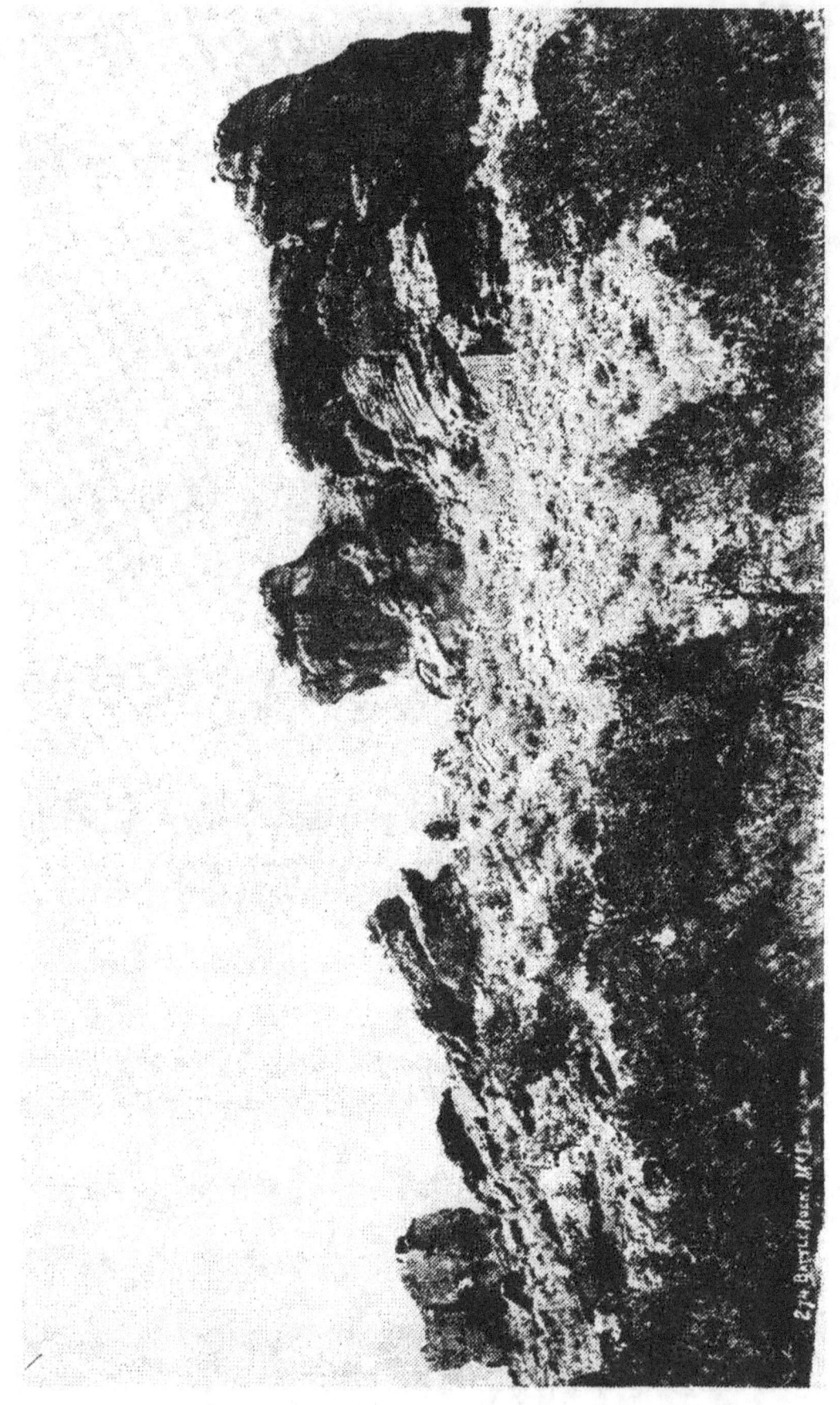

FIGURE 3. Circa 1875 photograph of surface pueblo in McElmo Canyon by W. H. Jackson. The caption on the photo is in error. The site is near but not on Battle Rock. Courtesy Smithsonian Institution National Anthropological Archives.

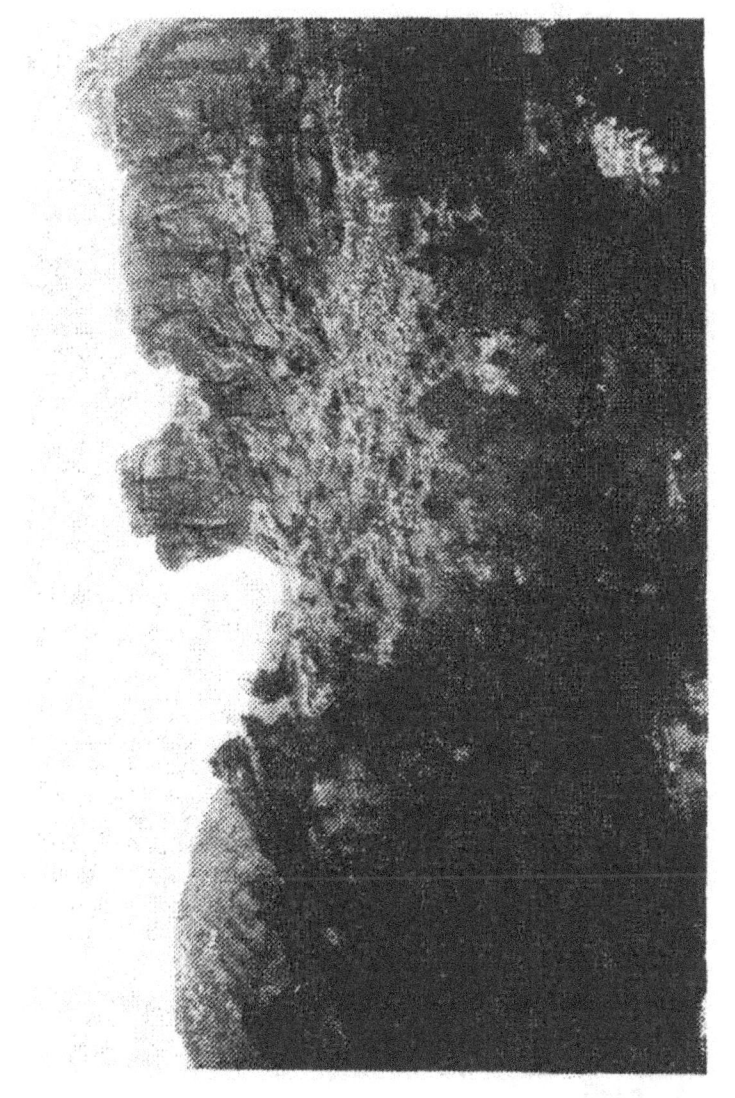

FIGURE 4. 1977 photograph of 5MT 1825, which is the same
site as Figure 3. This site is located near a modern road
and has suffered extremes in vandalism. Note the radical
changes between 1875 and 1977.

1923-24b   Further archaeological research in the northern San
            Juan Basin of Colorado, during the summer of 1922.
            Colorado Magazine 1(1):10-36, 1(5):213-224, 1(6):260-276,
            1(7):301-307.

Jennings, Calvin H.
    1966   Report on the excavation of three sites, Mesa Verde
            National Park, Colorado, 1965-1093, 1993, 60. Mesa
            Verde National Park, Colorado. xeroxed.

    1968a   Salvage excavations at sites 1094 and 1093, east fork
            of Navajo Canyon. In Contributions to Mesa Verde
            archaeology V, emergency archaeology in Mesa Verde
            National Park, Colorado, 1948-1966, edited by Robert
            H. Lister. University of Colorado Studies, Series in
            Anthropology, No. 15:45-52.

    1968b   Archaeological excavations at site 60, Chapin Mesa. In
            Contributions to Mesa Verde archaeology V, emergency
            archaeology in Mesa Verde National Park, Colorado,
            1948-1966, edited by Robert H. Lister. University of
            Colorado Studies, Series in Anthropology, No. 15:53-56.

    1968c   The Paleo-Indian and Archaic stages in western Colorado.
            Southwestern Lore 34(1):11-20.

Jennings, J. D.
    1940   A variation of Southwestern Pueblo culture. Laboratory
            of Anthropology, Technical Bulletin 10 (April).

Jennings, J. P., E. K. Reed, and others
    1956   The American Southwest: a problem in cultural isolation.
            Seminars in archaeology: 1955, edited by R. Wauchope.
            Society for American Archaeology, Memoir 11.

Jensen, Buddy Lee
    1975   Dolores River investigations, Ute Mountain Indian
            Reservation, Colorado and New Mexico. U.S. Department
            of the Interior, Fish and Wildlife Service, Gallup.
            xeroxed.

Jetl, Stephen C.
    1964   Pueblo Indian migrations: an evaluation of the possible
            physical and cultural determinants. American Antiquity
            29:281-300.

Johnson, H. J.
    1929   The Mesa Verde National Park. Colorado School of Mines
            Magazine (October).23-25, 38. Golden.

Jones, Volney H.
  1938   An ancient food plant of the Southwest and Plateau
              regions. El Palacio 44(5-6):41-53.

Jones, Volney H. and Robert L. Fonner
  1954   Plant materials from sites in the Durango and La Plata
              Areas, Colorado. In Basket Maker II sites near Durango,
              Colorado, by E. H. Morris and Robert F. Burgh. Carnegie
              Institution of Washington, Publication 604:93-116.

Jorde, L. B.
  1977   Precipitation cycles and cultural buffering in the
              prehistoric Southwest. In For theory building in
              archaeology. Essays on faunal remains, acquatic
              resources, spatial analysis, and system modeling,
              edited by Lewis K. Binford, pp. 385-396. Academic
              Press, New York.

Judd, Neil M.
  1924   Report on illegal excavations in Southwestern ruins.
              American Anthropologist 26:428-432.

Kaplan, Lawrence
  1956   The cultivated beans of the prehistoric Southwest.
              Annals of the Missouri Botanical Garden 43:189-251.

Kane, Allen G.
  1968a   Site 1677, two stone-lined pits and associated features.
              In Contributions to Mesa Verde archaeology V, emergency
              archaeology in Mesa Verde National Park, Colorado 1948-
              1966, edited by Robert H. Lister. University of Colorado
              Studies, Series in Anthropology, No. 15:101-103.

  1968b   Site 1925, a storage cist on Wetherill Mesa. In
              Contributions to Mesa Verde archaeology V. Emergency
              archaeology in Mesa Verde National Park, Colorado,
              1948-1966, edited by Robert H. Lister. University of
              Colorado Studies, Series in Anthropology, No. 15:105-106.

  1975a   Archaeological resources of the Dolores River Project.
              Report of the 1975 field season. University of Colorado
              Archaeological Research Center, Mesa Verde National Park,
              Colorado. xeroxed.

  1975b   Archaeological resources of the Dolores River Project.
              Report of the 1975 field season. Interagency Archaeological
              Services, National Park Service, Denver. xeroxed.

1975c   Archaeological resources in the Great Cut Dike - Dove Creek area, Dolores River Project. Report of the 1975 field season. Midwest Archaeological Center, National Park Service, Lincoln. xeroxed.

1977   Archaeological resources of the Dolores River Project. Report of 1976 operations. University of Colorado Archaeological Research Center, Mesa Verde National Park, Colorado. xeroxed.

Kane, Al, L. V. Nordby and T. Birkedal
1968   Cliff dwelling survey. Bureau of Indian Affairs, Albuquerque. xeroxed.

Karlstrom, Thor
1974   Paper presented at symposium on Mesa Verde, 1974 Pecos Conference, Mesa Verde National Park, Colorado.

Keating, M.
1907   Knowledge of ages is buried in Mesa Verde. Modern World 8. Baltimore.

Kent, Kate Peck
1957   The cultivation and weaving of cotton in the prehistoric southwestern United States. Transactions of the American Philosophical Society, new series 47 (part 3). Philadelphia.

Kidder, A. V.
1917   Prehistoric cultures of the San Juan drainage. Proceedings of the 19th International Congress of Americanists:108-113.

1923   Basket-Maker caves in the Mesa Verde. El Palacio 15:554-561.

1924   An introduction to the study of Southwestern archaeology. Yale University Press, New Haven.

1927   Southwestern archaeological conference. Science 66:489-491.

1962   An introduction to the study of Southwestern archaeology. Yale University Press, New Haven (first edition, 1924).

King, T. G.
1893   An exploration of the region occupied by the Cliff Dwellers. The Archaeologist 1:101-105.

Kunitz, Stephen J.
1970   Disease and death among the Anasazi. El Palacio 7(3):17-22.

Lafange, Christopher
     1945   Mesa Verde. The Vail Ballow Press, Inc., Binghampton,
                   N.Y.

Lancaster, James A.
     1940   Spruce Tree House. Waterproofing large crack in cave
                   roof. Mesa Verde National Park, Colorado. xeroxed.

     1941   Notes concerning the "Mummy Lake Ditch." Mesa Verde
                   National Park, Colorado. xeroxed.

     1948a   Salvage excavation of pithouses beside road, just
                   across from Twin Trees site. Mesa Verde National Park,
                   Colorado. xeroxed.

     1948b   Stabilization project of Pyge Shrine House. Mesa
                   Verde National Park, Colorado. xeroxed.

     1948c   Stabilization report: Square Tower House 1940, 1943,
                   1948. Mesa Verde National Park, Colorado. xeroxed.

     1949a   Report on inspection and stabilization of ruins at
                   Hovenweep National Monument. Mesa Verde National Park,
                   Colorado. xeroxed.

     1949b   Report on inspection and stabilization of ruins at Mesa
                   Verde National Park and stabilization of ruins at
                   Hovenweep National Monument. Mesa Verde National Park,
                   Colorado. xeroxed.

     1949c   Stabilization report: Hovenweep National Monument 1947,
                   1948, and 1949. Mesa Verde National Park, Colorado.
                   xeroxed.

     1949d   Stabilization report: Square Tower House and Spruce
                   Tree House 1934-1949. Mesa Verde National Park, Colorado.
                   xeroxed.

     1950a   Stabilization report: Far View 1941, 1942, 1950. Mesa
                   Verde National Park, Colorado. xeroxed.

     1950b   Stabilization report: House of Many Windows. Mesa
                   Verde National Park, Colorado. xeroxed.

     1950c   Stabilization report: Jug House. Mesa Verde National
                   Park, Colorado. xeroxed.

     1950d   Stabilization report: Sun Point Pueblo. Mesa Verde
                   National Park, Colorado. xeroxed.

1950e   Stabilization report: Sunset House. Mesa Verde National
           Park, Colorado. xeroxed.

1950f   Stabilization report: Sun Temple. Mesa Verde National
           Park, Colorado. xeroxed.

1950g   Stabilization report: ruin 16. Mesa Verde National
           Park, Colorado. xeroxed.

1950h   Stabilization report: site 16. Mesa Verde National
           Park, Colorado. xeroxed.

1950i   Stabilization report: site 515. Mesa Verde National
           Park, Colorado. xeroxed.

1950j   Stabilization report: site opposite Painted Kiva House.
           Mesa Verde National Park, Colorado. xeroxed.

1950k   Stabilization report: site 624. Mesa Verde National
           Park, Colorado. xeroxed.

19501   Stabilization report: site 636. Mesa Verde National
           Park, Colorado. xeroxed.

1950m   Stabilization report: site 628. Mesa Verde National
           Park, Colorado. xeroxed.

1951a   Stabilization report: Double House. Mesa Verde National
           Park, Colorado. xeroxed.

1951b   Stabilization report: Hovenweep National Monument 1948,
           1949 and 1951. Mesa Verde National Park, Colorado. xeroxed.

1951c   Stabilization report: Kodak House. Mesa Verde National
           Park, Colorado. xeroxed.

1951d   Stabilization report: Long House. Mesa Verde National
           Park, Colorado. xeroxed.

1951e   Stabilization report: Mummy House. Mesa Verde National
           Park, Colorado. xeroxed.

1951f   Stabilization report: Spring House. Mesa Verde National
           Park, Colorado. xeroxed.

1951g   Stabilization report: west side of Navajo Canyon opposite
           ASS. 583 Far View area 1951. Mesa Verde National Park,
           Colorado. xeroxed.

1954 Excavation of two late Basketmaker III pithouses.
     In Archaeological excavations in Mesa Verde National
     Park, Colorado, 1950, by James A. Lancaster and others.
     National Park Service Archaeological Research Series
     2:7-22.

Lancaster, James A. and Jean M. Pinkley
  1954 Excavation at site 16 of three Pueblo II mesa-top ruins.
     In Archaeological excavations in Mesa Verde National
     Park, Colorado, 1950, by James A. Lancaster and others.
     National Park Service Archaeological Research Series
     2:22-86.

Lancaster, James A., Jean M. Pinkley, Philip Van Cleve and Don Watson
  1954 Archaeological Excavations in Mesa Verde National Park
     Colorado, 1950. National Park Service Archaeological
     Research Series 2.

Lancaster, James A. and P. VanCleave
  1954 Excavation of Sun Point Pueblo. In Archaeological
     Excavations in Mesa Verde National Park, Colorado,
     1950, by James A. Lancaster and others. National
     Park Service Archaeological Research Series 2:87-111.

Lancaster, James A. and David A. Decker
  1961a Stabilization report: Cliff Palace. Mesa Verde
     National Park, Colorado. xeroxed.

  1961b Stabilization report: Twin Towers and Eroded Boulder
     House. Mesa Verde National Park, Colorado. xeroxed.

  1961c Stabilization report: site 529. Mesa Verde National
     Park, Colorado. xeroxed.

  1961d Stabilization report: Little Long House 1961. Mesa
     Verde National Park, Colorado. xeroxed.

  1963a Stabilization report: ruin 12 and site 1321. Mesa
     Verde National Park, Colorado. xeroxed.

  1963b Stabilization report: Stronghold House, Hovenweep
     National Monument. Mesa Verde National Park, Colorado.
     xeroxed.

  1963c Stabilization report: Horse Shoe House, Hovenweep
     National Monument. Mesa Verde National Park, Colorado.
     xeroxed.

  1963d Stabilization report: Cutthroat Castle, Hovenweep
     National Monument. Mesa Verde National Park, Colorado.
     xeroxed.

1952   Stabilization report: Pipe Shrine House 1942, 1949 and
            1952. Mesa Verde National Park, Colorado. xeroxed.

1955   Stabilization report: Far View. Mesa Verde National
            Park, Colorado. xeroxed.

1956a   Stabilization report: ASS #866. Mesa Verde National
            Park, Colorado. xeroxed.

1956b   Stabilization report: site 499. Mesa Verde National
            Park, Colorado. xeroxed.

1957   Stabilization report: Cutthroat Castle - 1957. Hovenweep
            National Monument. Mesa Verde National Park, Colorado.
            xeroxed.

1959a   Stabilization report: Cutthroat Castle, Hovenweep National
            Monument. Mesa Verde National Park, Colorado. xeroxed.

1959b   Stabilization report: site 875. Mesa Verde National
            Park, Colorado. xeroxed.

1967   Field notes for 1966-67 - restoration of Lowry Ruin.
            Mesa Verde National Park, Colorado. xeroxed.

1968a   The salvage excavation of sites 353 and 354, Chapin
            Mesa. In Contributions to Mesa Verde archaeology
            V, emergency archaeology in Mesa Verde National Park,
            Colorado, 1948-1966, edited by Robert H. Lister.
            University of Colorado Studies, Series in Anthropology,
            No. 15:57-60.

1968b   An archaeological test at site 80, Chapin Mesa. In
            Contributions to Mesa Verde Archaeology V, emergency
            archaeology in Mesa Verde National Park, Colorado,
            1948-1966, edited by Robert H. Lister. University of
            Colorado Studies, Series in Anthropology, No. 15:61-62.

Lancaster, J. A. and D. W. Watson
    1942a   Excavation of Mesa Verde pit houses. American Antiquity
            9(7):90-198.

    1942b   Excavations of the deep pithouses. Includes: Excavations
            of Mesa Verde pit houses (reprint) and Pithouse #1
            (reprint) by Terah Smiley. Mesa Verde National Park,
            Colorado. xeroxed.

1963e   Stabilization report: Unit House and ruin #11, Hovenweep
             National Monument. Mesa Verde National Park, Colorado.
             xeroxed.

1963f   Stabilization report: Holly Group, Hovenweep National
             Monument. Mesa Verde National Park, Colorado. xeroxed.

1963g   Stabilization report: Twin Towers, Hovenweep National
             Monument. Mesa Verde National Park, Colorado. xeroxed.

1963h   Stabilization report: Hackberry Group, Hovenweep
             National Monument. Mesa Verde National Park, Colorado.
             xeroxed.

1963i   Stabilization report: Hovenweep Castle and ruin #4,
             Hovenweep National Monument. Mesa Verde National Park,
             Colorado. xeroxed.

Lancaster, James A. and Leland J. Abel
    1968   Test excavation at site 391, a typical "burned rock area"
             on Chapin Mesa. In Contributions to Mesa Verde Archaeology
             V, emergency archaeology in Mesa Verde National Park,
             Colorado, 1948-1966, edited by Robert H. Lister. University
             of Colorado Studies, Series in Anthropology, No. 15:63-64.

Lang, Walter B.
    1937   Sun symbol markings. Journal of Washington Academy of
             Sciences 27(4):137-143.

Larralde, Signa
    n.d.   Perishables. In The Durango South Project: archaeological
             salvage of two late Basketmaker III sites in the Durango
             District, by John D. Gooding. Colorado Archaeological
             Society, Memoir (In press, ms. 1977).

Laubenfals, Max W.
    1942   Ecology of Mesa Verde National Park. Mesa Verde National
             Park Museum, Colorado. xeroxed.

Lavender, D.
    1936   Heaven and hell in the rim rock. Travel 67:11-13.

Laybourne, E. B.
    1932   The probable stature of the Cliff Dwellers. Mesa
             Verde Notes 3:17-19.

Leavesley, George H.
    1975   Quantity and quality of principal rivers entering the
             Southern Ute and Ute Indian Reservations, Colorado and
             New Mexico. U.S. Geological Survey, open-file report
             75-90. Denver.

Lee, Frank C.
  1938   Structure of Durango pre Kiva. Durango Public Library
              Museum Project 13:22-23. Durango.

Leh, Leonard L.
  1937   New explorations in archaeology. Colorado University
              Bulletin 37(15).

  1940   A prehistoric population center in the Southwest.
              Southwestern Lore 6(2):21-25.

Leidy, L. Kent
  1976   Archaeological resources of the Animas La Plata Project,
              report on the 1975 season. Interagency Archaeological
              Services, National Park Service, San Francisco. xeroxed.

Linton, Ralph
  1919   The small open ruins of the Mesa Verde. Mesa Verde
              National Park Archives, Bureau of American Ethnology,
              Washington, D. C. xeroxed.

  1944   Nomad raids and fortified pueblos. American Antiquity
              10(1):28-38.

Lister, Florence C. and Robert H. Lister
  1968   Earl Morris and Southwestern archaeology. University
              of New Mexico Press, Albuquerque.

Lister, Robert H.
  1964   Contributions to Mesa Verde archaeology I, site 499.
              University of Colorado Studies, Series in Anthropology,
              No. 9.

  1965   Contributions to Mesa Verde archaeology II, site 875,
              Mesa Verde National Park. University of Colorado Studies,
              Series in Anthropology, No. 11.

  1966a   Contributions to Mesa Verde archaeology III, site 866
              and the cultural sequence at four villages in the Far
              View group, Mesa Verde National Park, Colorado. University
              of Colorado Studies, Series in Anthropology, No. 12.

  1966b   Progress report upon the 1966 inventory of archaeological
              remains in lands controlled by the Bureau of Land Management
              in the Cortez - Dove Creek area of southwestern Colorado.
              Bureau of Land Management, Denver. xeroxed.

  1967a   Progress report upon the 1967 inventory of archaeological
              remains in lands controlled by the Bureau of Land Management
              in the Cortez - Dove Creek area of southwestern Colorado.
              Bureau of Land Management, Denver. xeroxed.

1967b   Contributions to Mesa Verde archeology IV, site 1086, an isolated, above ground kiva in Mesa Verde National Park, Colorado. <u>University of Colorado Studies, Series in Anthropology</u>, No. 13.

1968a   Archaeology for layman and scientist at Mesa Verde. <u>Science</u> 160:8.

1968b   Contributions to Mesa Verde archaeology V, emergency archaeology in Mesa Verde National Park, Colorado, 1948-1966. <u>University of Colorado Studies, Series in Anthropology</u>, No. 15.

1968c   Progress report upon the 1968 inventory of archaeological remains in lands controlled by the Bureau of Land Management in the Cortez - Dove Creek area of southwestern Colorado. Bureau of Land Management, Denver. xeroxed.

1969a   Environment and Man in Mesa Verde. <u>Naturalist</u> 20(2):1-37.

1969b   University of Colorado Archaeological Research Center. <u>Naturalist</u> 20(2):1-45.

Lister, Robert, Joyce Herold, and Arthur Rohn
    1959   Site 52:an unusual PIII ruin on Mesa Verde. Mesa Verde National Park, Colorado. xeroxed.

Lister, Robert H. and David A. Breternitz
    1968   The salvage excavations of site 1104, Wetherill Mesa. In Contributions to Mesa Verde archaeology V, emergency archaeology in Mesa Verde National Park, Colorado, 1948-1966, edited by Robert H. Lister. <u>University of Colorado Studies, Series in Anthropology</u>, No. 15:69-88.

    n.d.   Survey notes on Bureau of Land Management survey on Cajon Mesa. Hovenweep National Monument. xeroxed.

Lister, Robert H. and Jack E. Smith
    1968   Salvage excavations at site 1088, Morfield Canyon. In Contributions to Mesa Verde archaeology V, emergency archaeology in Mesa Verde National Park, Colorado, 1948-1966, edited by Robert H. Lister. <u>University of Colorado Studies, Series in Anthropology</u>, No. 15:5-32.

Lister, Robert H. and Florence C. Lister
    1969   The Earl H. Morris Memorial Pottery Collection. <u>University of Colorado Studies, Series in Anthropology</u>, No. 16.

Lister, Robert H., Stephen J. Hallisey, Margaret H. Kane and
          George E. McClellen
     1970   Site 5LPII, a Pueblo I site near Ignacio, Colorado.
               Southwestern Lore 35(4):57-67.

Litzinger, William J.
     1976a   The experimental garden project 1975. In Hovenweep
               1975, by Joseph C. Winter. San Jose State University
               Archeological Report, No. 2:117-190.

     1976b   Plant zones of the Hovenweep area, Cajon Mesa, Colorado-
               Utah. In Hovenweep 1975, by Joseph C. Winter. San Jose
               State University Archeological Report, No. 2:215-238.

Lloyd, Carl
     1938   Expedition to Southwest finds another prehistoric village.
               Field Museum News 9(10):1.

Look, Al
     1951   In my backyard. University of Denver Press, Denver.

Lotrich, Victor F.
     1939   Shortened - barb type arrowhead. Colorado Magazine
               16(6):210-212.

Love-dePeyer, Barbara
     n.d. a   Chipped Stone Tools. In The Durango South Project:
               archaeological salvage of two late Basketmaker III sites
               in the Durango District, by John D. Gooding. Colorado
               Archaeological Society, Memoir (In press, ms. 1977).

     n.d. b   Shell beads. In The Durango South Project:archaeological
               salvage of two late Basketmaker III sites in the Durango
               District, by John D. Gooding. Colorado Archaeological
               Society, Memoir (In press, ms. 1977).

Luebben, Ralph A., Laurance Herold, and Arthur Rohn
     1957   Site 52 Mesa Verde National Park. Mesa Verde National
               Park, Colorado. xeroxed.

     1960   An unusual Pueblo III ruin, Mesa Verde, Colorado.
               American Antiquity 26(1):11-20.

Luebben, Ralph, Arthur Rohn, and R. Dale Owens
     1962   A partially subterranean Pueblo III structure. El Palacio
               69(3):225-239.

Luper, M. A.
     1977   Analysis of modified bones from site 5MTUMR2785 in the
               Mancos Canyon on the Ute Mountain Indian Reservation. In
               Excavations at site 5MTUMR2785, Mancos Canyon, Ute Mountain
               Homelands, Colorado, by Steven Emslie, Appendix C. Unpub-
               lished M.A. thesis. Department of Anthropology, University
               of Colorado, Boulder.

Lucas, Ken
    1972   A preview at Mesa Verde's Mug House. <u>Popular Archaeology</u>
                1(3):4-9.

McClellen, George
    1966   Ute pasture survey. Mesa Verde Research Center, Mesa
                Verde National Park, Colorado. xeroxed.

    1969   The origin, development and typology of Anasazi great
                kivas. Unpublished Ph.D. dissertation. Department of
                Anthropology, University of Colorado, Boulder.

McClellan, George E. and Stephen J. Hallisey
    1970   Salvage excavation of 5MRUMR1268 in Mancos Canyon, Ute
                Mountain Reservation, Colorado. <u>Southwestern Lore</u>
                35(4):68-75.

McClurg, V. G. and G. McClurg
    1917   The development of the Mesa Verde National Park. <u>Travel</u>
                27:34-37. New York.

McCoy, Robert
    1960   Peoples of the Mesa Verde. <u>National Parks Magazine</u> 34:158.

McGregor, J. C.
    1965   <u>Southwestern archaeology.</u> University of Illinois Press,
                Urbana.

McIntyre, Allan
    1977   Soil chemistry studies of Hov. 24. In Hovenweep 1976,
                by Joseph C. Winter. <u>San Jose State University Archeo-
                logical Report, No.</u> 3:151-158.

McKern, W. C.
    1924   Western Colorado petroglyphs. Bureau of American Ethnology,
                Manuscript 106. Washington, D. C.

McLoyd, Charles and C. C. Graham
    1894   Catalogue of cliff house and cavern relics - Durango,
                Colorado. Reviewed in the <u>Archaeologist</u> 2:184.

McNitt, Frank
    1957   <u>Richard Wetherill: Anasazi.</u> University of New Mexico
                Press, Albuquerque.

McWhirt, Jean
    1939   Esther. <u>Mesa Verde Notes</u> 9(1):1-5.

MacClary, J. S.
    1927   The first American farmers. Art and Archaeology 24:83-88. Baltimore and Washington, D. C.

Macomb, J. N.
    1876   Report of the exploring expedition from Santa Fe, New Mexico to the junction of the Grand and Green Rivers of the West in 1859. Government Printing Office, Washington, D. C.

Maher, Louis J. Jr.
    1963   Pollen analysis of surface material from the southern San Juan Mountains, Colorado. The Geological Society of American, Bulletin 74:1485-1584.

Maher, Thomas M.
    1966   Mesa Verde, the prehistoric Cliff Dwellers and the effect of the supernova of 1054 A.D. Tri State Printing Co., Cincinnati.

Markham, C. R.
    1894   American Cliff Dwellers. Geographical Journal 3:46-47. London.

Marquart, Cynthia
    1968   Basic data on early sites in Colorado and adjacent regions. Southwestern Lore 34(1):21-30.

Marriot, Alice
    1952   Indians of the Four Corners. Thomas Y. Crowell Co., New York.

Martin, Curtis
    1976   Archaeological inventory of the Sand Canyon cliff dwelling area, Montezuma County, Colorado. Bureau of Land Management, Montrose. xeroxed.

Martin, Daniel W., Robert H. Lister and David A. Breternitz
    1971   Evaluation of the archaeological resources on public lands of the Bureau of Land Management in the Cortez - Dove Creek area (McElmo district) of southern Colorado. Bureau of Land Management, Montrose. xeroxed.

Martin, Paul Sidney
    1927   The Pecos Conference on Southwest archaeology. Colorado Magazine 4(14):180-182.

    1929   The 1928 archaeological expedition of the State Historical Society of Colorado. Colorado Magazine 6(1):1-35.

1929-30   Archaeological expedition of the State Historical Society
           of Colorado in cooperation with the Smithsonian Institution.
           Colorado Magazine 7(1):1-40.

1930b   Archaeological expedition to the Southwest. Field
           Museum News 1(11):3.

1930c   Kiva revealed on Lowry Ruin. Field Museum News 1(19):1.

1931a   Expedition to the Southwest returns with collections.
           Field Museum News 2(11):3.

1931b   Recent archaeological excavations in southwestern
           Colorado. Pan American Magazine 44(3):228-236.

1933   Expedition to the Southwest returns with collections.
           Field Museum News 4(11):2.

1938a   Ancient Colorado village and temple uncovered. Field
           Museum News 9(9):3.

1938b   Expedition to Southwest ends successful season. Field
           Museum News 9(11):3.

1939   Excavations of 1938: Basketmaker sites in southwestern
           Colorado. Pan American Traveler 1(2):38-39. Lake
           Charles, New York.

1947   Indians before Columbus, Part IV: the Southwest, section
           12. In The Anasazi culture, by George Quimby and Donald
           Collier. University of Chicago Press, Chicago.

1968   Lowry Pueblo, then and now. Field Museum of Natural
           history, Bulletin 39(4).

1974   Lowry Ruin and the Anasazi culture. In Archaeological
           series, research in retrospect, edited by C. W. Willey
           and J. Sabloff, pp. 8-12. Winthrop Publishing Co. Inc.,
           Cambridge.

Martin, Paul S., Lawrence Roys, and Gerhardt Von Bonin
     1936   Lowry Ruin in southwestern Colorado. Field Museum of
               Natural History Anthropological Series 23(1).

Martin, Paul S., Carl Lloyd and Alexander Spoehr
     1938   Archaeological work in the Ackmen-Lowry area, southwestern
               Colorado, 1937. Field Museum of Natural History 23(2).

Martin, Paul S. and John Rinaldo
1939   Modified Basketmaker sites Ackmen-Lowry area southwestern
         Colorado, 1938. Field Museum of Natural History Anthro-
         pological Series 23(3).

Martin, Paul S. and Elizabeth S. Willis
1940   Anasazi painted pottery in Field Museum of Natural History.
         Field Museum of Natural History Anthropology Memoirs 5.

Martin, Paul Shultz
1973   The last 10,000 years: a fossil pollen record of the
         American Southwest. University of Arizona Press, Tucson.

In Press Pollen stratigraphy of Long House. National Park Service,
          Washington, D.C.

Martin, Paul S. and Floyd W. Sharlock
1964   Analysis of prehistoric human feces: a new approach
         to ethnobotany. American Antiquity 30:168-180.

Martin, Paul Shultz and William Byers
1965   Pollen and archaeology at Wetherill Mesa. In Contributions
         of the Wetherill Mesa Archaeological Project, assembled
         by Douglas Osbourn. Society for American Archaeology,
         Memoir 19:122-135.

Maslin, T. P.
1959   An annotated checklist of the amphibians and reptiles
         of Colorado. University of Colorado Studies, Series
         Biological 6.

Mason, C. C.
1918   The story of the discovery and early exploration of the
         cliff houses at the Mesa Verde. State Historical Society
         of Colorado, Denver. xeroxed.

Mason, O. T.
1904   Aboriginal American basketry. U.S. National Museum,
         Annual Report for 1902:171-548.

Masterson, Kellie
1975   Basketry remains from Johnson Canyon, Colorado. In
         The 1974 Johnson-Lion Canyon Project: report of
         investigation, assembled by Paul R. Nickens, pp. 223-
         239. Bureau of Indian Affairs, Albuquerque. xeroxed.

Mather, S. T.
1920   Mesa Verde, the gateway to the Pacific National Parks.
         Mid Pacific Magazine 20:340-344. Honolulu.

Mathews, Meridith H.
    1976   Botanical remains recovered from fire pits at 5MTUMR2785:
                a Pueblo site in Mancos Canyon Colorado. In Excavations
                at Site 5MTUMR2785, Mancos Canyon, Ute Mountain Ute
                Homelands, Colorado, by Steven Emslie, Appendix.
                Unpublished M.A. thesis. Department of Anthropology,
                University of Colorado, Boulder.

Mesa Verde National Park
    1974   Final environmental impact statement FES 74-24 proposed
                Mesa Verde National Park wilderness. Mesa Verde National
                Park, Colorado. xeroxed.

Messinger, Norman
    1965   Methods used for identification of feather remains from
                Wetherill Mesa. American Antiquity 31(2):206-215.

Miles, James S.
    1966   Diseases encountered at Mesa Verde, Colorado. In Human
                paleontology by Saul Jarcho, pp. 91-97. Yale University
                Press, New Haven.

    1975   Orthopedic problems of the Wetherill Mesa populations.
                National Park Service Publications in Archaeology,
                No. 7-G.

Milford, Stanley J.
    1940   A San Juan burial. El Palacio 47(11):1-235.

Miller, William C. and David A. Breternitz
    1958   1958 Navajo Canyon survey preliminary report. Plateau
                31(1):3-7.

Mindeleff, C.
    1898   Origin of the cliff dwellings. Bulletin of American
                Geographical Society 30(2):111-123. New York.

    1901   A cliff dwelling park in Colorado. Scientific American
                81:297-298.

Minnis, Paul E. and Richard I. Ford
    1977   Analysis of plant remains from Chimney Rock Mesa. In
                Archaeological investigations at Chimney Rock Mesa;
                1970-1972, by Frank W. Eddy. Colorado Archeological
                Society, Memoir 1:81-91.

Mitchell, Winnifred
    1971   An archaeological test at site MV1966. A small surface
                pueblo on Long Mesa, Mesa Verde National Park, Colorado.
                Mesa Verde National Park, Colorado. xeroxed.

1972a   Three small structures on Wetherill Mesa: Sites MV
         1582, MV1560, and structure 4 of MV1937. Midwest
         Archaeological Center, National Park Service, Lincoln.
         xeroxed.

1972b   Three isolated fire pits on Wetherill Mesa. Midwest
         Archaeological Center, National Park Service, Lincoln.
         xeroxed.

Mornat, A. D.
    1944   Annual growth of pines in the San Juan basin as related
            to precipitation and stream flow. Tree Ring Bulletin
            10:29-30.

Monroe, Arthur W.
    1950   Silent water. Wetsel Publishing Co., Inc., New York.

Montogomery, Ross
    1940   Archaeological pot hunting. Master Key 14:28-29.

Moorehead, Dean
    1939   The Developmental Pueblo diorama. Mesa Verde Notes
            9(1).

Moorehead, Warren K.
    1892   The great ruins of upper McElmo Creek. Illustrated
            American.

Moorehead, W. K. and L. W. Gunkel
    1892   In search of a lost race. Illustrated American 10:116,
            11:119, 121, 122, 124-130. New York.

More, Lucy
    1937   Excavation. Mesa Verde Notes 7(1).

Morgan, A.
    1876-77   On the cliff houses and antiquities of southwestern
               Colorado and New Mexico. The Literary and Philosophical
               Society of Liverpool Proceedings (66th Session):346-356.
               Liverpool.

Morgan, L. H.
    1881a   Houses and house life of the American aborigines. Contri-
             butions to North American Ethnology 10:72. Washington,
             D. C.

    1881b   Ruins of houses of the sedentary Indians of the San Juan
             River and its tributaries. Contributions to North American
             Ethnology 4:154-197. Washington, D. C.

Morgan, W. F.
  1879   Description of a cliff house on the Mancos River of
            Colorado, with a ground plan. American Association
            for the Advancement of Science Proceedings 27:300-306.

Morley, Sylavanus G.
  1908   The excavation of the Cannonball Ruins in southwestern
            Colorado. American Anthropologist 10(4):596-610.

Morley, S. G. and A. V. Kidder
  1917   The archaeology of McElmo Canyon Colorado. El Palacio
            4:41-70.

Morris, Earl H.
  1919   Preliminary account of the antiquities of the region
            between the Mancos and LaPlata River in southwestern
            Colorado. Bureau of American Ethnology, 33rd Annual
            Report:155-206.

  1921   Chronology of the San Juan area. National Academy of
            Sciences Proceedings 7:18-22.

  1927   The beginnings of pottery making in the San Juan area,
            unfired prototypes and the wares of the earliest ceramic
            period. American Museum of Natural History Anthropological
            Papers 28 (part 2).

  1934   Speaker chief's house. Mesa Verde Notes 5(1):1-4.

  1939   Archaeological studies in the LaPlata District, south-
            western Colorado and northwestern New Mexico. Carnegie
            Institute of Washington, Publication 519:1-298.

  1949   Basket Maker II dwellings near Durango, Colorado. Tree
            Ring Bulletin 15:33-34.

  1952   Note on the Durango dates. Tree Ring Bulletin 18:36.

  n.d.   LaPlata ruins. American Museum of Natural History
            17(7):481.

Morris, E. H. and Robert F. Burgh
  1941   Anasazi basketry BMIII - PIII, a study based on specimens
            from the San Juan River. Carnegie Institute of Washington,
            Publication 535.

  1954   Basketmaker II sites near Durango, Colorado. Carnegie
            Institute of Washington, Publication 604.

Muench, David
    1974   Anasazi: ancient people of the rock. American West,
                Palo Alto.

Nemetz, Judith A.
    1977   Archaeological excavations at the Escalante site, Dolores,
                Colorado, 1975 and 1976. Unpublished M.A. thesis. Depart-
                ment of Anthropology, University of Colorado, Boulder.

Newberry, J. S.
    1876   Geological report in J. N. Macomb report of the exploring
                expedition from Santa Fe, New Mexico, to the junction
                of the Grand and Green Rivers of the West in 1859.
                Government Printing Office, Washington, D. C.

Newell, F. H.
    1898   Mesa Verde, National Geographic 9:431-434.

Nichols, Robert F.
    1962   Dates from site 1060 pithouse, Mesa Verde National Park.
                Tree Ring Bulletin 24:12-14.

Nichols, Robert F. and Thomas Harlan
    1967   Archaeological tree ring dates from Wetherill Mesa.
                Tree Ring Bulletin 28(1-6):13-40.

Nickens, Paul R.
    1974a   Analysis of prehistoric human skeletal remains from the
                Mancos Canyon, southwestern Colorado. Bureau of Indian
                Affairs, Albuquerque. xeroxed.

    1974b   Additional human skeletal remains from the Mancos Canyon,
                southwestern Colorado. Department of Anthropology,
                University of Colorado, Boulder. xeroxed.

    1975a   The 1974 Johnson-Lion Canyon Project: report of
                investigation I. Bureau of Indian Affairs, Albuquerque.
                xeroxed.

    1975b   Cannibalism in the Mancos Canyon, southwestern Colorado.
                Kiva 40:283-293.

    1975c   Human skeletal remains from the 1974 University of Colorado
                Mancos Canyon excavations. In Preliminary report of
                excavations at the Ute Canyon Site, 5MTUMR2347, Ute
                Mountain Ute Homelands, Colorado, by William B. Gillespie,
                pp. 138-156. Bureau of Indian Affairs, Albuquerque.
                xeroxed.

1975d   Osteological analysis of five human burials from Mesa
Verde National Park, Colorado. <u>Southwestern Lore</u>
41:13-26.

1975e   Paleoepidemiology of Mesa Verde Anasazi populations:
lines of increased density. Department of Anthropology,
University of Colorado, Boulder. xeroxed.

1975f   The Johnson-Lion Canyon Project: environmental archaeology
in southwestern Colorado (abstract). <u>Journal of the
Colorado-Wyoming Academy of Science</u> 7(6):1.

1976a   An archaeological survey of the Johnson Canyon area,
southwestern Colorado. In Johnson-Lion Canyon Project:
report of investigation II. Bureau of Indian Affairs,
Albuquerque. xeroxed.

1976b   Paleoepidemiology of Mesa Verde Anasazi populations:
lines of increased density (abstract). <u>Journal of the
Colorado-Wyoming Academy of Science</u> 8(1):4-5.

1976c   The Johnson-Lion Canyon Project: report of investigation
III. Bureau of Indian Affairs, Albuquerque. xeroxed.

1977   Environment and adaption of Johnson Canyon, southwestern
Colorado: Pueblo III communities in transition. Unpub-
lished Ph.D. dissertation. Department of Anthropology,
University of Colorado, Boulder.

n.d.   Pollen samples submitted for analysis from Hoy House
(5MTUMR2150) Johnson Canyon, southwestern Colorado.
Department of Anthropology, University of Colorado,
Boulder. xeroxed.

Noisat, Bradley A.
1975   Water control at Hovenweep, appendix III. In Hovenweep
1974, edited by Joseph Winter. <u>San Jose State University
Archaeological Report</u>, <u>No.</u> 1:147-151.

1976a   Water control experimentation. In Hovenweep 1975, by
Joseph C. Winter. <u>San Jose State University Archeological
Report</u>, <u>No.</u> 2:191-196.

1976b   The soils of Hovenweep. In Hovenweep 1975, by Joseph C.
Winter. <u>San Jose State University Archeological Report</u>,
<u>No.</u> 2:270-281.

61

Nordby, Larry V.
    1973   Salvage excavations in Mancos Canyon, Ute Mountain Ute
                Homelands during the Summer of 1972. Unpublished M.A.
                thesis. Department of Anthropology, University of
                Colorado, Boulder.

    1974   The excavation of sites 5MTUMR2343, 5MTUMR2345, 5MTUMR2346,
                Mancos Canyon, Ute Mountain Ute Homelands, Colorado.
                Bureau of Indian Affairs, Albuquerque. xeroxed.

    n.d.   Supplementary testing at site 5MTUMR2346. Ute Mountain
                Ute Homelands, Colorado. Bureau of Indian Affairs,
                Albuquerque. xeroxed.

Nordby, Larry V. and David A. Breternitz
    1972   Site MV1824-71, a Basketmaker III pithouse and cist on
                Wetherill Mesa. Midwest Archaeological Center, National
                Park Service, Lincoln. xeroxed.

Nordenskiold, Gustaf
    1895   The Cliff Dwellers of the Mesa Verde, southwestern
                Colorado; their pottery and implements. Norstedt and
                Stones, Stockholm, Sweden.

Nusbaum, Deric
    1926   Deric in Mesa Verde. Putman Sons, Knicker Bocker Press,
                New York.

    1928   Ancient rattle found by Deric Nusbaum. El Palacio
                24(15):277-280.

Nusbaum, Jesse L.
    1911   The excavation and repair of Balcony House, Mesa Verde
                National Park (abstract). American Journal of Archaeology
                (2nd Series) 15:75. Corcord, New Hampshire.

    1922   Mesa Verde National Park. American Forestry 28:408-409.
                Washington, D. C.

    1949   The 1926 reexcavation of Step House Cave: Mesa Verde
                National Park. Mesa Verde National Park Museum, Colorado.
                xeroxed.

Nusbaum, Jesse and Earl Morris
    1935   La Plata valley survey diary, attribute list of pottery.
                Mesa Verde National Park, Colorado. xeroxed.

O'Bryan, Deric
    1950   Excavations in Mesa Verde National Park, 1947-48.
                Medallion Papers 39:1-144.

1967   Climate and tree rings in the Mesa Verde. National
            Parks Magazine 41(235):17-19.

Olsen, Nancy Hulbert
    1977   Hovenweep rock art and agriculture. In Hovenweep 1976,
                by Joseph C. Winter. San Jose State University
                Archeological Report, No. 3:279-292.

Osbourn, Carolyn M.
    1965   The preparation of yucca fiber: an experimental study.
                In Contributions of the Wetherill Mesa Archaeological
                Project, assembled by D. Osbourn. Society for American
                Archaeology, Memoir 19:45-50.

    n.d.   Notes on wood artifacts from Long House, Wetherill Mesa
                Project. Mesa Verde National Park, Colorado. xeroxed.

Osbourn, Douglas
    1964   Wetherill Mesa yields secrets of the Cliff Dwellers.
                National Geographic 125(2):155-211.

    1965a   Chipping remains as an indication of cultural change
                at Wetherill Mesa. In Contributions of the Wetherill
                Mesa Archaeological Project, edited by D. Osbourn.
                Society for American Archaeology, Memoir 19:30-44.

    1965b   Contributions of the Wetherill Mesa Archaeological Project.
                Society for American Archaeology, Memoir 19.

    1966   The sites: the archaeological background at Mesa Verde.
                In Human paleontology, edited by Saul Jarcho, pp. 85-87.
                New Haven and London.

    1976   Slow exodus from Mesa Verde. Natural History 85(1):38-45.

Osbourn, Douglas, and others
    1967   The dendrochronology of the Wetherill Mesa Archaeological
                Project. Tree Ring Bulletin 28(1-4).

Parsons, Elsie C.
    1906   The Mesa Verde National Park. American Antiquarian
                28:256-266. New York.

    1917   Cliff dwellings of the Mesa Verde. Railroad Red Book
                (June):21-23. Denver.

    1921   Cliff Dwellers of the Mesa Verde. Travel 14:5-14. New
                York.

Peabody, W. A.
    1907   Mesa Verde National Park. Modern World 8:159-163.
                Baltimore.

Peet, S. D.
    1890   The Cliff Dwellers and their works. American Antiquarian
                12:85-104. New York.

    1896   A study of the high cliff dwellings and cave towns.
                American Antiquarian 18:285-302. New York.

    1898a   Caves and cliff dwellings compared. American Antiquarian
                20:193-211. New York.

    1898b   Cliff fortresses. American Antiquarian 20:80-100.
                New York.

    1898c   Great houses and fortresses. American Antiquarian
                20:315-338. New York.

    1898d   The Cliff Palace and its surroundings. American
                Antiquarian 20:19-36. New York.

Pendergast, David M. (Editor)
    1961   Ecological studies of the flora and fauna of the Navajo
                Reservoir Basin, Colorado and New Mexico. University
                of Utah Anthropological Papers, No. 55.

Pendleton, Michael and Dorothy Washburn
    1977   Comparative analysis of the surface treatment of Pueblo
                II-III Corrugated Wares from Hovenweep National Monument.
                In Hovenweep 1976, by Joseph C. Winter. San Jose State
                University Archeological Report, No. 3:79-92.

Penn, Mark
    1977   Human skeletal remains from site 2785. In Excavations
                at site 5MRUMR2785, Mancos Canyon, Ute Mountain Ute
                Homelands, Colorado, by Steven Emslie, Appendix D.
                Unpublished M.A. thesis. Department of Anthropology,
                University of Colorado, Boulder.

Peterson, Kenneth L. and Peter J. Mehringer, Jr.
    1976   Postglacial timberline fluctuations, La Plata mountains,
                southwestern Colorado. Artic and Alpine Research
                8(3):275-288.

Petsche, J. E.
    1968   Bibliography of salvage archaeology in the United States.
                Publications in Salvage Archaeology, No. 10. River Basin
                Surveys, Museum of Natural History, Smithsonian Institution.

Pike, Donald
    1973   The people who have vanished. American West 10(6):40-47.

Pinkley, Jean M.
    1958   The Mesa Verde experimental cornfield. Mesa Verde
                National Park Museum, Colorado. mimeographed.

    1965   The Pueblos and the turkey: who domesticated whom.
                In Contributions of the Wetherill Mesa Archaeological
                Project, assembled by Douglas Osbourn. Society for
                American Archaeology, Memoir 19:70-72.

Pinkley, Nancy M.
    1931   Ten sixty-six to thirteen hundred. Mesa Verde Notes
                2(2):1-19.

Plog, Fred T. and Cheryl K. Garrett
    1972   Explaining variability in prehistoric Southwestern water
                control systems. In Contemporary archaeology, edited by
                Mark P. Leone, pp. 280-288. Southern Illinois University,
                Carbondale.

Prudden, T. Mitchell
    1896   A summer among cliff dwellings. Harpers New Monthly
                Magazine 93:545-561.

    1897   An elder brother of the Cliff Dweller. Harpers Monthly
                95:56-63.

    1901   Glimpses of the Great Plateau. Harpers New Monthly
                Magazine 103:745-750.

    1903   The prehistoric ruins of the San Juan watershed in Utah,
                Arizona, Colorado, and New Mexico. American Anthropologist
                5:224-288.

    1907   On the Great American Plateau. G. P. Putnam's Sons,
                New York.

    1914   The circular kivas of small ruins in the San Juan water-
                shed. American Anthropologist 16:23-58.

    1918   A further study of prehistoric small house ruins in the
                San Juan watershed. American Anthropological Association,
                Memoir 5:3-50.

Rado, Theodore
    1975   A preliminary faunal study of Hovenweep National Monument.
                In Hovenweep 1974, by Joseph C. Winter. San Jose State
                University Archeological Report, No. 1:137-146.

1976   An evaluation of potential prehistoric faunal resources on Cajon Mesa, Utah. In Hovenweep 1975, by Joseph C. Winter. San Jose State University Archeological Report, No. 2:239-251.

Reagan, A. B.
1919   The ancient ruins in lower and middle Pine River valley, Colorado. El Palacio 7:171-176.

1922   Archaeological notes on Pine River valley, Colorado 1916-20. Kansas Academy of Science Transactions 30:244-250.

Reaves, Dorothy
1977   Hovenweep maize 1974-1976. In Hovenweep 1976, by Joseph C. Winter. San Jose State University Archeological Report, No. 3:232-236.

Reed, Alan D.
1975   Bone artifacts of the Johnson Canyon area of southwestern Colorado. In The 1974 Johnson-Lion Canyon Project: report of investigation I, assembled by Paul R. Nickens, pp. 57-90. Bureau of Indian Affairs, Albuquerque. xeroxed.

1976   An analysis of the quids from Hoy House and Lion House. In The Johnson-Lion Canyon Project: report of investigations III, assembled by Paul R. Nickens, pp. 145-182. Bureau of Indian Affairs, Albuquerque. xeroxed.

1977   The Dominguez Ruin: a McElmo Phase site in southwestern Colorado. Unpublished M.A. thesis. Department of Anthropology, University of Colorado, Boulder.

Reed, Alan D. and Ronald E. Kainer
n.d.   The Tamarron site: a Basketmaker II site in southwestern Colorado. Southwestern Lore (In press, ms. 1977).

Reed, C., G. Wood, A. Wanek, and P. MacKee
1947   Stratigraphy and geological structure in the Piedra River canyon, Archuleta County, Colorado. United States Geological Survey, Oil and Gas Investigations, Preliminary Map A6.

Reed, Erik K.
1939   The enemy people. In Our own Spanish American citizens and the Southwest which they colonized. Coronado Cuatro Centennial 1(Article 5). U.S. Department of the Interior, Washington, D. C.

1944a   An archaeological study of Mancos Valley, southwestern
         Colorado and its position in the prehistory of the
         American Southwest. Unpublished Ph.D. thesis. Harvard
         University, Cambridge.

1944b   The abandonment of the San Juan Region. El Palacio
         51:4.

1946   The distinctive features and distribution of the San
         Juan Anasazi culture. Southwestern Journal of Anthropology
         2:295-305.

1948   Archaeological work in Mancos Canyon, Colorado. American
         Antiquity 10:48-58.

1949a   Sources of upper Rio Grande Pueblo culture and population.
         El Palacio 56(6):163-184.

1949b   The significance of skull deformation in the Southwest.
         El Palacio 56:106-119.

1951   Types of stone axes in the Southwest. Southwestern Lore
         17(3):45-51.

1956   Human skeletal remains from archaeological surveys of
         New Mexico and Colorado. In Pipeline archaeology, reports
         of salvage operations in the Southwest on El Paso Natural
         Gas Company Project 1950 #53, edited by Fred Wendorf,
         pp. 393-401. Laboratory of Anthropology, Santa Fe.

1958   Excavations in Mancos Canyon, Colorado. University of
         Utah Anthropological Papers, No. 35.

1962   Pine trees. Pollen and climatic history of the Southwest.
         National Park Service Regional Research Abstract, No. 292.
         Santa Fe.

1963   The period known as Pueblo. National Park Service Regional
         Research Abstract, No. 304. Santa Fe.

1965   Human skeletal material from site 34, Mesa Verde National
         Park. El Palacio 72:31-45.

Reiter, Paul
    1946   Form and function in some prehistoric ceremonial structures
            in the Southwest. Unpublished Ph.D. dissertation.
            Harvard University, Cambridge.

Renaud, E. B.
1925   The Indians of Colorado. University of Colorado Studies. Boulder.

1927   Undeformed prehistoric skulls from La Plata (Colorado) and Canyon Del Muerto Arizona. University of Colorado Studies 16:8-16. Boulder.

1931   Prehistoric flaked points from Colorado and neighboring districts. Proceedings of the Colorado Museum of Natural History 10:6-17.

1935   The archaeological survey of Colorado, fourth report, seasons 1933-34. University of Denver. mimeographed.

1936a   Pictographs and petroglyphs of Colorado I. Southwestern Lore 2:57-60.

1936b   Racial mixture of the Mesa Verde Indians. Southwestern Lore 1:3-5.

1937   Pictographs and petroglyphs of Colorado II-V. Southwestern Lore 2:74-79, 3:12-19, 35-40, 45-48.

1941   Western and Southwestern Indian skulls. University of Denver Anthropological Series, First Paper.

Retzius, G.
1893   Human remains from the Cliff Dwellers of the Mesa Verde. Norstedt and Soner, Stockholm, Sweden.

Reyman, Jonathan Eric
1975   Mexican influence on Southwestern ceremonialism. Xerox University of Microfilms, Ann Arbor.

Rhoda, Franklin
1877   Topographical report on the Southwestern district. In United States Geological and Geographical Survey of the Territories, 9th Annual Report, by F. V. Hayden, pp. 302-333.

Richardson, G. N.
1893   The early Americans. California Illustrated Magazine 4:774-783.

Richert, Roland and Gordon Vivian
1962   Handbook for ruins stabilization part 2, field methods. National Park Service, Washington, D.C.

1974   Ruins stabilization in southwestern United States. National Park Service, Washington, D.C.

Rife, D. W.
1931   Primitive Man's diet in the Mesa Verde area. Mesa Verde Notes 2:17-18.

Riley, Carrol
1948a   An archaeological survey at Hovenweep National Monument. Unpublished M.A. thesis. Hovenweep National Monument, Colorado.

1948b   An archaeological survey at Hovenweep National Monument, Revised Summer 1948. Hovenweep National Monument, Colorado. xeroxed.

1950   Defensive structures in the Hovenweep Monument. El Palacio 57:339-344.

Rinaldo, John
1939   Artifacts. In Modified Basketmaker sites Ackmen-Lowry area, southwestern Colorado, 1938, by Paul S. Martin and John Rinaldo. Field Museum of Natural History Anthropological Series 23(3).

1941   An analysis of prehistoric Anasazi culture change. Unpublished Ph.D. dissertation. University of Chicago.

1950   An analysis of culture change in the Ackmen-Lowry area. Fieldiana 36(5):93-106.

Ripley, Don
1961a   Hovenweep, the deserted valley. Utah Archaeology 7(1):15-17.

1961b   The deserted valley. Master Key 35(2):1-60.

Ripley, Don and Ruth Simpson
1961   The deserted valley and a visit to Hovenweep National Monument. Master Key 35(2):60-63.

Roberts, Frank H. H. Jr.
1922   Report on the work of the 1922 season in the Piedra Parada archaeological field. University of Denver, Bulletin 23:1-12.

1924   Pre-Columbian cultures, house types and their distribution in the state of Colorado. Department of Anthropology, University of Denver. xeroxed.

1925   Report on archaeological reconnaissance in southwestern
Colorado in the summer of 1923. <u>Colorado Magazine</u> 2(2):
1-80.

1929   Exploration and field work of the Smithsonian Institution
in certain early Pueblo villages in southwestern Colorado.
<u>Smithsonian Miscellaneous Collections</u> 81(7):161-168.

1930   Early Pueblo ruins in the Piedra District, southwestern
Colorado. <u>Bureau of American Ethnology, Bulletin</u> 96.

1935   A survey of Southwestern archaeology. <u>American Antiquity</u>
37:1-35.

1946   Prehistoric peoples of Colorado. <u>Colorado Magazine</u>
23(445):145-156, 215-230.

1947   Archaeology in the Southwest. <u>American Antiquarian</u>
3(3):33. New York.

n.d.   The Smithsonian Institution and the Southwest. In The
significance of the Coronado Cuatro Centennial. <u>Coronado
Quatro Centennial</u> 2 (Article 1).

Roberts, F. H. H. and J. A. Jeancon
1921   Archaeological report in the northeastern San Juan basin
of Colorado in the summer of 1921 (abstract). Colorado
State Historical Society, Denver. xeroxed.

Robinson, Christine
1976a   Temporal change in lithic material from the Mesa Verde
Region. Department of Anthropology, University of
Colorado, Boulder. xeroxed.

1976b   Human skeletal remains from 1975 archaeological excavations
in Mancos Canyon, Colorado. Unpublished M.A. thesis.
Department of Anthropology, University of Colorado,
Boulder.

Robinson, William J. and Jeffrey S. Dean
1969   Tree-ring evidence for climatic changes in the prehistoric
Southwest from A.D. 1000-1200. 1967-1968 annual report
to the National Park Service. Laboratory of Tree Ring
Research, Tucson. xeroxed.

Robinson, William J. and Bruce G. Harrill
1974   <u>Tree ring dates from Colorado V: Mesa Verde area.</u>
<u>Laboratory of Tree Ring Research, Tucson.</u>

Rodeck, Hugo G.
 1954a   Earl Morris and the University of Colorado Museum. An
          appreciation. Southwestern Lore 12:32-39.

 1954b   Animal and bird bones from the Durango site. In
          Basketmaker II sites near Durango, Colorado, by E. H.
          Morris and Robert F. Burgh. Carnegie Institution of
          Washington, Publication 604:117-121.

Rohn, Arthur H.
 1959   A tentative classification of pottery from the Mesa Verde
          Region. Mesa Verde National Park, Colorado. mimeographed.

 1963a   An ecological approach to the Great Pueblo occupation of
          the Mesa Verde, Colorado. Plateau 36(1):1-17.

 1963b   Prehistoric soil and water conservation on Chapin Mesa
          southwestern Colorado. American Antiquity 28(4):441-445.

 1965   Postulation of socio economic groups from archaeological
          evidence. In Contributions of the Wetherill Mesa
          Archaeological Project, assembled by D. Osbourn. Society
          for American Archaeology, Memoir 19:65-69.

 1966   Cultural continuity and change on Chapin Mesa, south-
          western Colorado. Unpublished Ph.D. dissertation. Harvard
          University, Cambridge.

 1971   Mug House Mesa Verde National Park - Colorado. National
          Park Service Archaeological Research Series 7D.

 1972   Social implications of water management in the Northern
          San Juan. Sonderdruk:Zeitschrift for Ethnologie, Bund
          97, Heft 2.

 1974   Payne site investigations. Southwestern Lore 40(3 and 4):
          50-52.

 1975   A stockaded Basketmaker III village at Yellowjacket,
          Colorado. Kiva 40(3):113-120.

 1977   Cultural change and continuity on Chapin Mesa. Regents
          Press of Kansas, Lawrence.

 n.d.   Social organization from settlement patterns in the
          Northern San Juan. Mesa Verde National Park, Colorado.
          xeroxed.

Rohn, Arthur H. and Jervis D. Swannack, Jr.
    1965   Mummy Lake Gray: a new pottery type. In Contributions
                of the Wetherill Mesa Archaeological Project, assembled
                by D. Osbourn. Society for American Archaeology, Memoir
                19:14-18.

Ross, Kenneth
    1936   Lowry Ruin as an introduction to the study of Southwestern
                masonry. In Lowry Ruin in southwestern Colorado, by
                P. S. Martin. Field Museum of Natural History Anthro-
                pological Series 23(1):115-142.

    1937   A tree looks at life. Mesa Verde Notes 7(1).

Rowen, Edward J., III
    n.d. a   Human skeletal remains from the Tamarron site, 5LP326.
                Southwestern Lore (In press, ms. 1977).

    n.d. b   Human skeletal remains. In The Durango South Project:
                archaeological salvage of two late Basketmaker III sites
                in the Durango District, by John D. Gooding. Colorado
                Archaeological Society, Memoir (In press, ms. 1977).

Sabels, Bruno E.
    n.d.   Manganese and phosphorus abundances in Wetherill Mesa
                feces and soils with some implications concerning the
                prehistory of Mesa Verde Cliff Dwellers. Desert Research
                Institute, University of Nevada. xeroxed.

Samuels, Robert
    1965   Parasitological study of long-dried fecal samples.
                In Contributions of the Wetherill Mesa Archaeological
                Project, assembled by D. Osbourn. Society for American
                Archaeology, Memoir 19:175-179.

Schaafsma, Curtis
    1974   Archaeological clearance survey of Colorado State
                Highway 184, between Mancos and Dolores. Office of
                the State Archaeologist, Denver. xeroxed.

Schaafsma, Curtis and John D. Gooding
    1974a   Archaeological survey between Mancos and Dolores, U.S.
                Highway 184, Colorado Department of Highways Project No.
                RS 0184(2). Highway Salvage Report No. 4.

    1974b   Archaeological survey of U.S. Highway 160-550 Durango
                South. Colorado State Highway Department. Project No.
                F019-2(14). Highway Salvage Report, No. 8.

Schaafsma, Polly
    1965   Southwest Indian pictographs and petroglyphs. Museum of
                New Mexico Press, Albuquerque.

Schmeckebier, L. F.
    1912   Our National Parks. <u>National Geographic</u> 23:531-519.

Schmoll, Hazell
    1932   Vegetation of the Chimney Rock area, Pagosa-Piedra
                region, Colorado. Unpublished Ph.D. dissertation.
                University of Chicago Library, Chicago.

    1935   <u>Vegetation of the Chimney Rock area, Pagosa-Piedra</u>
                <u>region, Colorado</u>. University of Chicago Library,
                Chicago.

Schoenwetter, James
    1966   A reevaluation of the Navajo Reservoir pollen chronology.
                <u>El Palacio</u> 73:19-26.

    1970   Archaeological pollen studies of the Colorado Plateau.
                <u>American Antiquity</u> 35(1):35-48.

Schoenwetter, James and Frank Eddy
    1964   Alluvial and palynological reconstruction of environments,
                Navajo Reservoir District. <u>Museum of New Mexico Papers</u>
                <u>in Anthropology</u>, <u>No.</u> 13.

Schoenwetter, James and Alfred E. Dittert, Jr.
    1968   An ecological interpretation of Anasazi settlement
                patterns. In <u>Anthropological archaeology in the</u>
                <u>Americas</u>, edited by Betty J. Meggers, pp. 41-66. The
                Anthropological Society of Washington, D. C.

Schroeder, Albert H. and James A. Lancaster
    1964   Report on test excavations at Yucca House. Mesa Verde
                National Park, Colorado. xeroxed.

Schroeder, Albert H.
    1967a   An archaeological survey adjacent to Hovenweep National
                Monument. <u>Southwestern Lore</u> 33(3 and 4):61-94.

    1967b   Themes of environmental adaptation and response in
                Southwestern National Park System areas. <u>Southwestern</u>
                <u>Lore</u> 33(2):37-46.

Schulman, Albert
    1950   Pre-Columbian towers in the Southwest. <u>American</u>
                <u>Antiquity</u> 15(4):288-297.

Schulman, Edmund
    1946   Dendrochronology at Mesa Verde National Park. <u>Tree</u>
                <u>Ring Bulletin</u> 12(3):18-24.

1947 An 800 year Douglas fir at Mesa Verde. <u>Tree Ring Bulletin</u> 14(1):2-8.

1949a Early chronologies in the San Juan basin. <u>Tree Ring Bulletin</u> 15:24-32.

1949b An extension of the Durango chronology. <u>Tree Ring Bulletin</u> 16(1):12-16.

1952 Extension of the San Juan chronology to B.C. times. <u>Tree Ring Bulletin</u> 18:35.

Sciscenti, James V., Alfred E. Dittert Jr., and Beth Dickey
1963a Excavations at the Martinez site, LA4104. In Pueblo period sites in the Piedra River Section, Navajo Reservoir District, assembled by Alfred E. Dittert, Jr. and Frank W. Eddy. <u>Museum of New Mexico Papers in Anthropology</u>, <u>No.</u> 10:112-122.

1963b Excavations at the Martinez site, LA4134. In Pueblo period sites in the Piedra River Section, Navajo Reservoir District, assembled by Alfred E. Dittert, Jr. and Frank W. Eddy. <u>Museum of New Mexico Papers in Anthropology</u>, <u>No.</u> 10.

1963c Excavations at the Railroad site, LA4103. In Pueblo period sites in the Piedra River District, assembled by Alfred E. Dittert, Jr. and Frank W. Eddy. <u>Museum of New Mexico Papers in Anthropology</u>, No. 10:80-111.

Scott, Douglas D.
1972 The Nordenskiold campsite: a test in historic archaeology. <u>Kiva</u> 37(3):128-140.

1977 Two vandalized Pueblo III burials: some key factors affecting vandalism of sites. <u>Southwestern Lore</u> 43(3): 10-14.

Scott, Linda J.
1974a Palynological analysis of sites 5MRUMR2343 and 5MTUMR2346. Department of Anthropology, University of Colorado, Boulder. xeroxed.

1974b Palynological analysis of site 5MTUMR2344. Department of Anthropology, University of Colorado, Boulder. xeroxed.

1976 Hoy House: a palynological study. In The Johnson-Lion Canyon Project: report of investigation III, assembled by Paul R. Nickens, pp. 8-49. Bureau of Indian Affairs, Albuquerque. xeroxed.

1977a   A study of ethnobotanic pollen from 5MTUMR2785 Mancos Canyon Colorado. In Excavations at site 5MTUMR2785 Mancos Canyon, Ute Mountain Ute Homelands, Colorado, by Steven D. Emslie, Appendix A. Unpublished M.A. thesis. Department of Anthropology, University of Colorado, Boulder.

1977b   Pollen analysis of Dominguez Ruin. Department of Anthropology, University of Colorado, Boulder. xeroxed.

1978   An analysis of pollen, 5MTUMR2837, Mancos Canyon, Colorado. Department of Anthropology, University of Colorado, Boulder. xeroxed.

n.d.   Pollen analysis of Mummy Lake. Department of Anthropology, University of Colorado, Boulder. xeroxed.

Sender, Malcolm K.
1975   Footwear recovered from the cliff dwellings in Johnson Canyon, southwestern Colorado. In The 1974 Johnson-Lion Canyon Project: report of investigation I, assembled by Paul R. Nickens, pp. 240-290. Bureau of Indian Affairs, Albuquerque. xeroxed.

Sheets, John
1977   Facial asymmetry and artificial cranial deformation in a set of American Indian skulls. Southwestern Lore 43(3):15-21.

Sheets, Payson D. and Terje G. Birkedal
1968   Site 1107, a small Pueblo II unit on Wetherill Mesa. In Contributions to Mesa Verde archaeology V, emergency archaeology in Mesa Verde National Park, Colorado, 1948-1966, edited by Robert H. Lister. University of Colorado Studies, Series in Anthropology, No. 15:89-94.

Shelse, R. C.
1922a   Mesa Verde Cliff Dwellers. Mazama 10:1-12. Portland, Oregon.

1922b   Mesa Verde Cliff Dwellers. Mintor 10(5):3-12. New York.

Shephard, Anna O.
1939   Technology of the La Plata pottery. In Archaeological studies in the La Plata district, by Earl H. Morris. Carnegie Institute of Washington, Publication 519:249-288.

1948   The symmetry of abstract design with special reference
        to ceramic decoration. Contributions to American
        Anthropology and History, No. 47:217-292.

1957   Ceramics for the archaeologist. Carnegie Institute
        of Washington, Publication 609.

Shoemaker
1912   Cliff dwellings of Colorodo. Travel 19:16-19. New York.

Short, Glen B.
1969   A report on the human skeletal remains from the Mesa
        Verde 820 site of southwestern Colorado. Department
        of Anthropology, University of Colorado, Boulder. xeroxed.

Short, Susan K.
1972   Analysis of bulk soil samples, Chimney Rock, Colorado,
        1970 and 1971. Department of Anthropology, University
        of Colorado, Boulder. xeroxed.

1975   Pollen analysis at Chimney Rock, Colorado: 5AA88 and
        tuffy traps. In 1972 archaeological explorations at
        the Ravine site, Chimney Rock, Colorado, by Marcia
        Truell, Appendix A. Unpublished M.A. thesis. Department
        of Anthropology, University of Colorado, Boulder.

n.d.   Pollen analysis, 5LP110 and 5LP111, Durango, Colorado.
        In The Durango South Project: archaeological salvage of
        two late Basketmaker III sites in the Durango District,
        by John D. Gooding. Colorado Archaeological Society,
        Memoir (In press, ms. 1977).

Simpson, Ruth
1961   A visit to Hovenweep National Monument. Master Key
        35(2):63-68.

Smidt, John Lancaster
1970   Population dynamics of mule deer in Mesa Verde National
        Park. Unpublished Ph.D. dissertation. Colorado State
        University, Ft. Collins.

Smiley, Terah
1947   Dates from a surface pueblo at Mesa Verde. Tree Ring
        Bulletin 13(4):30-32.

1949   Pithouse number I, Mesa Verde National Park. American
        Antiquity 14(3):167-171.

1950   Miscellaneous ring records, II. Tree Ring Bulletin
        16(3):22-23.

1951   A summary of tree ring dates from some Southwestern archaeological sites. <u>Laboratory of Tree Ring Research, Bulletin</u> 5.

Smith, H. J.
1893   <u>The Cliff Dwellers</u>. Chicago World's Columbian Exposition, Jay Smith Exploring Company. Mesa Verde National Park, Colorado. xeroxed.

Smith, H. M., T. P. Maslin, and R. L. Brown
1965   Summary of the distribution of the herpetofauna of Colorado. <u>University of Colorado Studies, Series in Biology, No.</u> 15.

Smith, Jack
1967   Tower survey summer 1967, conducted by Jack Smith and George E. McClellan. Mesa Verde National Park, Colorado. xeroxed.

1972   Archaeological survey of Mesa Verde National Park, 1971 season. Mesa Verde National Park, Colorado. xeroxed.

1973a   Archaeological survey of Mesa Verde National Park, 1972 season. Mesa Verde National Park, Colorado. xeroxed.

1973b   Summary of the 1971-1972 seasons of the Mesa Verde, archaeological survey. Midwest Archaeological Center, National Park Service, Lincoln. xeroxed.

1974   Archaeological survey of Mesa Verde National Park, 1973 season. Mesa Verde National Park, Colorado. xeroxed.

1975   Archaeological survey of Mesa Verde National Park, 1974 season. Mesa Verde National Park, Colorado. xeroxed.

1976   Archaeological survey of Mesa Verde National Park, 1975 season. Mesa Verde National Park, Colorado. xeroxed.

1977   Archaeological survey of Mesa Verde National Park, 1976 season. Mesa Verde National Park, Colorado. xeroxed.

n.d.   The story of Mesa Verde National Park. In <u>Denver and Rio Grande Western R. R. Co.</u> Denver.

Smith, K. L.
1902   The preservation of cliff dwellings. <u>Overland Monthly</u>, (2nd Series) 30:875-881. San Francisco.

Smithsonian Institution
1917   Prehistoric remains in New Mexico, Colorado and Utah. Smithsonian Miscellaneous Collections 66:76-92.

Snyder, J. F.
1897   The Cliff Dwellers sandal last. Antiquarian 1:128-130. Columbus.

1899   The sandal last of the Cliff Dwellers. American Archaeologist 35-9. Columbus.

Spencer, L. W.
1928   Cliff Dweller lands. Art and Archaeology 25:285-291. Baltimore and Washington, D. C.

Spoehr, Alexander
1949   Southwestern pithouses. American Antiquity 15(1):55.

Stallings, W. Jr.
1937   Southwestern dated ruins. Tree Ring Bulletin 4(1):3.

Stephenson, Robert L.
1967   Frank H. H. Roberts Jr., 1897-1966. American Antiquity 32:84-94.

Stevenson, Joy Brown
1975   Technological analysis of prehistoric cotton textiles from Mancos Canyon and associated environmental considerations. In The 1974 Johnson-Lion Canyon Project: report of investigations I, assembled by Paul R. Nickens, pp. 91-141. Bureau of Indian Affairs, Albuquerque. xeroxed.

Stewart, Bruce
1967   Park point. All Points Bulletin, Newsletter of the Denver Chapter, Colorado Archaeological Society 4(12):3-6.

Stewart, Guy R.
1933   Archaeological problems of northern periphery southwest United States. Museum of Northern Arizona, Bulletin 5.

1940   Conservation in Pueblo agriculture. Scientific Monthly 51:201-220, 329-340.

n.d.   Conservation practices in flood water agriculture at Mesa Verde. Mesa Verde National Park, Colorado. xeroxed.

Stewart, G. R. and Maurice Donnelly
1943a   Soil and water economy in the Pueblo Southwest, I. Scientific Monthly 56(51 and 52):31-44, 134-44, New York.

1943b   Soil and water economy in the Pueblo Southwest, II.
             Evaluation of primitive methods of conservation.
             Scientific Monthly 56:134-144. Lancaster, New York.

Stewart, Omer C.
    1947   Archaeology, ethnology and history in Colorado. South-
             western Lore 13:24-28.

    1971   Ethno-historical bibliography of the Ute Indians of
             Colorado. University of Colorado Studies, Series in
             Anthropology, No. 18.

Stewart, T. D.
    1937   Different types of cranial deformity in the Pueblo area.
             American Anthropology 39:169-171.

Stiger, Mark A.
    1975a   The coprolites of Hoy House: a preliminary analysis
             (abstract). Journal of the Colorado - Wyoming Academy
             of Science 7.

    1975b   The coprolites of Hoy House: a preliminary analysis.
             In The 1974 Johnson-Lion Canyon Project: report of
             investigations I, assembled by Paul R. Nickens, pp.
             142-153. Bureau of Indian Affairs, Albuquerque. xeroxed.

    1976   The application of microtechnique to the analysis of
             coprolites. In The Johnson-Lion Canyon Project: report
             of investigations III, assembled by Paul R. Nickens.
             Bureau of Indian Affairs, Albuquerque. xeroxed.

    1977   Anasazi diet: the coprolite evidence. Unpublished M.A.
             thesis. Department of Anthropology, University of
             Colorado, Boulder.

Sutton, V.
    1937   The sutures of the Mesa Verde Cliff Dwellers. Mesa
             Verde Notes 7:1-2.

Swannack, Jervis D., Jr.
    1969   Big Juniper House, Mesa Verde National Park, Colorado.
             National Park Service Archeological Research Series 7 E.

Swedland, Alan Charles
    1969   Human skeletal material from the Yellow Jacket Canyon
             area, southwestern Colorado. Unpublished M.A. thesis.
             Department of Anthropology, University of Colorado, Boulder.

Sweet, S. L.
    1924   A conservation lesson from the Cliff Dwellers. American
                Forests and Forest Life 30:654-657.

Swift, Marilyn
    1977   Hovenweep lithic sources. In Hovenweep 1976, by Joseph
                C. Winter. San Jose State University Archeological Report,
                No. 3:170-182.

Switzer, Ronald K.
    1974   The effects of forest fire on archaeological sites in
                Mesa Verde National Park, Colorado. The Artifact 12(3):1-8.
                El Paso Archaeological Society, Inc.

Tatum, R. N.
    1942   Petroglyphs of southern Colorado. Trinidad State Junior
                College Science Series, No. 2.

Taylor, Walter W.
    1954   Southwestern archaeology: its history and theory.
                American Anthropologist 56:561-570.

The Colorado Society of the Archaeological Institute of America
    1908   Announcement of fieldwork, season of 1908. Bureau
                of Land Management. Montrose. xeroxed.

Thompson, A. H.
    1904   Ruins of the Mesa Verde Topekan's explorations among
                the ancient cities of the Cliff Dwellers. Topeka
                Daily Herald:July 21.

    1905   Ruins of the Mesa Verde. American Antiquarian 27:6-8.

Thompson, C.
    n.d.   Exterior ornamentation on Mesa Verde bowls. Mesa Verde
                Notes 3:40-43.

Thurman, Ray
    1960   Our trip to Mesa Verde. Central States Archaeological
                Journal 7:10-16. Quincy, Ill.

Tobin, Samuel J.
    1947   Archaeology in the San Juan. University of Utah
                Anthropological Papers, No. 8:95-108.

    1950   Notes on site number 1, Cahone Ruin, southwestern Colorado.
                Southwestern Lore 15(4):46-50.

Toll, Henry W. III
    1974   Archaeological resources in the Dolores River canyon
              below the proposed McPhee Reservoir, Montezuma, Dolores,
              and San Miguel Counties Colorado. Bureau of Land Manage-
              ment, Montrose. xeroxed.

    1976a   Dolores River archaeology 1975 survey and synthesis.
              Unpublished M.A. thesis. Department of Anthropology,
              University of Colorado, Boulder.

    1976b   Quartzite: the poor cousin in lithic analysis. Depart-
              ment of Anthropology, University of Colorado, Boulder.
              xeroxed.

    1977   Dolores River archeology: canyon adaptations as seen
              through survey. Bureau of Land Management Cultural
              Resource Series, No. 4. Denver.

Tower, Donald B.
    1945   The use of marine mollusca and their value in reconstructing
              prehistoric trade routes in the American Southwest. Papers
              of the Excavators Club 2(3):1-56.

Truell, Marcia
    1972   Chimney Rock Archaeological Project: preliminary report
              1972 summer excavations. National Forest Service, San
              Juan National Forest, Durango. xeroxed.

    1973   1972 archaeological explorations at site 88 at Chimney
              Rock-the building 16 complex and structure 17. National
              Forest Service, San Juan National Forest, Durango. xeroxed.

    1975   1972 archaeological explorations at the Ravine site,
              Chimney Rock Colorado. Unpublished M.A. thesis. Depart-
              ment of Anthropology, University of Colorado, Boulder.

Turney, Christy B.
    1962   A summary of the archaeological explorations of Dr. Byron
              Cummings in the Anasazi culture area. Papers of the
              Museum of Northern Arizona, Technical Series 5.

Bureau of Indian Affairs, Ignacio
    1965   Soil and range inventory of the Ute Mountain Indian
              Reservation, Colorado and New Mexico. Branch of Land
              Operations, Phoenix Area Office. xeroxed.

    1966   Soil and range inventory, Southern Ute Reservation,
              Colorado. Branch of Roads, Phoenix Area Office. xeroxed.

1968   Cliff Dwellers survey, Lister Project. Ute Mountain
            Indian Reservation. xeroxed.

United State Forest Service
    1971   Dolores Project, environmental impact summary report.
            Rocky Mountain Region, Denver.

United States National Park Service
    1938   Mesa Verde National Park Colorado. U.S. Department of
            Interior, Washington, D.C.

    n.d.   Hovenweep - Colorado and Utah. Mesa Verde National Park,
            Colorado. xeroxed.

U.S, Soil Conservation Service
    1972   General soil map, Montezuma County, Colorado. U.S.
            Department of Agriculture, Portland, Oregon.

University of Colorado, Boulder
    1965-1970 Site reports on survey in San Juan area - 14 Vols.
            Bureau of Land Management, Montrose. xeroxed.

Valdez, Norbert
    n.d.   Cultural implications of prehistoric maize remains from
            Johnson Canyon, southwestern Colorado. M.A. thesis (in
            preparation). University of Idaho, Moscow.

VanCleave, Philip F. (Assembler)
    n.d.   Mesa Verde tree ring data. Mesa Verde National Park,
            Colorado. xeroxed.

Vivian, R. Gordon
    1959   The Hubbard site and other tri-wall structures in New
            Mexico and Colorado. National Park Service Archaeological
            Research Series 5.

Vivian, Gordon and Paul Reiter
    1965   The great kivas of Chaco Canyon and their relationships.
            School of American Research, Monograph 22.

Vivian, R. Gwinn
    1974   Conservation and diversion: water control systems in the
            Anasazi Southwest. In Irrigation's impact on society,
            edited by T. E. Downing and McQuire Gibson. University
            of Arizona Anthropological Papers, No. 25:95-112.

Von Bonin, Gerhard H.
    1936   Skeletal material from the Lowry area. In Lowry Ruin
            in southwestern Colorado, by Paul S. Martin, Carl Lloyd,
            and Alexander Spoehr. Field Museum of Natural History
            Anthropological Series 23(1).

82

Wade, William D., and George J. Armelagos
    1966   Anthropometrical data and observations upon human skeletal
                material. In Contributions to Mesa Verde archaeology III
                site 866, and the cultural sequence at four villages in
                the Far View group, Mesa Verde National Park, Colorado,
                by R. H. Lister. University of Colorado Studies, Series in
                Anthropology, No. 12:97-112.

Wanek, A. A.
    1954   Geologic map of the Mesa Verde area Montezuma County,
                Colorado. Oil and Gas Investigations Map OM152. U.S.
                Geological Survey.

    1959   Geology and fuel resources of the Mesa Verde area,
                Montezuma and La Plata Counties, Colorado. U.S. Geological
                Survey, Bulletin 100.1072-M.

Ward Williams, Linda
    1976   Cultural resource inventory report for the Dolores Ranger
                District, Pagosa Springs Ranger District, Mancos Ranger
                District. U.S. Forest Service, San Juan National Forest,
                Durango. xeroxed.

Warren, E. R.
    1942   The mammals of Colorado. University of Oklahoma Press,
                Norman.

Washburn, Dorothy K.
    1975   Ceramic analysis. In Hovenweep 1974, by Joseph C. Winter.
                San Jose State University Archeological Report, No. 1:50-62.

    1976a   Ceramic analysis. In Hovenweep 1975, by Joseph C. Winter.
                San Jose State University Archaeological Report, No. 2:9-20.

    1976b   Symmetry analysis of design on black-on-white pottery from
                Hovenweep National Monument. In Hovenweep 1975, by Joseph C.
                Winter. San Jose State University Archeological Report,
                No. 2:21-35.

    1976c   Objects of unknown use and ornaments. In Hovenweep 1975,
                by Joseph C. Winter. San Jose State University Archeological
                Report, No. 2:70-75.

Watson, Don
    1934   Museum acquisitions for 1934. Mesa Verde Notes 5(1).

    1935   Museum acquisitions for 1935. Mesa Verde Notes 6(1):1-5.

    1937   The Cliff Dwellers visit the dentist. Mesa Verde Notes 7:7-10.

1939   The excavation of pit house number 1. Mesa Verde National Park, Colorado. xeroxed.

1940   Cliff Palace, the story of an ancient city. Edwards Brothers, Ann Arbor, Mich.

1947   Note on the dating of Pipeshrine House. Tree Ring Bulletin 13(4):32.

1951   Cliff dwellings of the Mesa Verde. Mesa Verde Museum Association, Mesa Verde National Park, Colorado.

1953   Indians of the Mesa Verde. Mesa Verde Museum Association, Mesa Verde National Park, Colorado.

1954   Introduction to Mesa Verde archaeology. In Archaeological excavations in Mesa Verde National Park, Colorado, 1950, by James A. Lancaster and others. National Park Service Archaeological Research Series 2:1-6.

Watson, Don, James A. Lancaster, and Leland J. Abel
1968   Archaeological salvage at sites 1030 and 1066, Prater Canyon. In Contributions to Mesa Verde archaeology V, emergency archaeology in Mesa Verde National Park, Colorado, 1948-1964, edited by Robert H. Lister. University of Colorado Studies, Series in Anthropology, No. 15:33-36.

Weber, William A.
1967   Rocky Mountain flora. University of Colorado Press, Boulder.

Weir, Glendon H.
1976   Preliminary pollen analysis of Hovenweep area archaeological sediments. In Preliminary report: Hovenweep 1975, by Joseph C. Winter, pp. 40-55. Mesa Verde National Park, Colorado. xeroxed.

1977   Pollen evidence for environmental change at Hovenweep National Monument AD 900-AD 1300. In Hovenweep 1976, by Joseph C. Winter. San Jose State University Archeological Report, No. 3:246-278.

Welsh, Stanley L. and James A. Erdman
1964   Annotated checklist of the plants of Mesa Verde, Colorado. Brigham Young University Science Bulletin, Biological Series 4(2).

Weltfish, G.
1932   Prehistoric basketry of Hovenweep National Monument. Smithsonian Miscellaneous Collections 87:12-16.

Wendorf, Fred C.
    1956   Pipeline archaeology, reports of salvage operations in the
                Southwest on El Paso Natural Gas Company Project 1950 #53.
                Laboratory of Anthropology, Santa Fe.

Wenger, Gilbert R.
    1969   Archaeological research at Mesa Verde National Park.
                Naturalist 20(2):1-27.

Wenger, Oswald
    n.d.   Report on archaeology. Mesa Verde National Park, Colorado.
                xeroxed.

Wenger, Stephen R.
    1976   Flowers of the Mesa Verde National Park. Mesa Verde Museum
                Association, Mesa Verde National Park, Colorado.

West, G. A.
    1932   A visit to Mesa Verde. Milwaukee Public Museum Year Book
                10:27-44.

Weston, Timothy
    1975   A functional analysis of bone tools from Mancos Canyon
                Colorado. Mesa Verde Research Center, Mesa Verde National
                Park, Colorado. xeroxed.

    1978   The archaeology of Moccasin Mesa, Mesa Verde National Park,
                Colorado. Unpublished M.A. thesis. Department of Anthro-
                pology, University of Colorado, Boulder.

Wetherill, B. A.
    1931   How I found the Mesa Verde ruins. Travel 23:30-35, 54.
                New York.

Wetherill, Richard
    1879   Letters to the editor, Antiquarian 1:248.

    1894a   Sniders Well. Archaeologist 2(9):288-289. Waterloo, Ind.

    1894b   Letter containing a description of a painted kiva found
                at Sniders Ranch, Montezuma County, Colorado. Archaeologist.

    1897   The sandal stones. Antiquarian 1:2-48.

Wheat, Joe Ben
    1955   MT-1 Basketmaker III site near Yellowjacket, Colorado.
                Southwestern Lore 21(2):18-26.

1963   Prehistoric people of the northern Southwest. <u>Grand
Canyon Natural History Association, Bulletin</u> 12.

Wheat, Joe Ben, James C. Gifford, and William W. Wasley
1958   Ceramic variety, type cluster, and ceramic system in
Southwestern pottery analysis. <u>American Antiquity</u>
24(1):34-47.

Wheller, Richard P.
1965   Edge-abraded flakes, blades and cones, in the Puebloan
tool assemblage. In Contributions of the Wetherill Mesa
Archaeological Project, assembled by D. Osbourn. <u>Society
of American Archaeology, Memoir</u> 19:30-44.

n.d.   Stone artifacts and minerals. Wetherill Mesa report,
chapter five. Mesa Verde National Park, Colorado. xeroxed.

White Adrian S.
1976a   Analysis of wood artifacts from Johnson Canyon. In The
Johnson-Lion Canyon Project: report of investigation III,
assembled by Paul R. Nickens, pp. 183-253. Bureau of
Indian Affairs, Albuquerque. xeroxed.

1976b   Stabilization of Escalante Ruin - 5MT2149, Dolores, Colorado.
Bureau of Land Management, Montrose. xeroxed.

White, Adrian S. and David A. Breternitz
1976   Stabilization of Lowry Ruins. <u>Bureau of Land Management
Cultural Resource Series, No.</u> 1. Denver.

White, Clayton M. and William H. Behle
1961   Birds of Navajo Reservoir Basin in Colorado and New Mexico.
In Ecological studies of the flora and fauna of Navajo
Reservoir Basin, Colorado and New Mexico, edited by Angus
M. Woodbury. <u>University of Utah Anthropological Papers,
No.</u> 55:129-154.

White, Leslie A. (Editor)
1942   Lewis H. Morgans journal of a trip to southwestern Colorado
and New Mexico, June 21 to August 7, 1878. <u>American Antiquity</u>
8(1):1-26.

White, Thomas D.
1976   Faunal remains. In Hovenweep 1975, by Joseph C. Winter.
<u>San Jose State University Archeological Report, No.</u> 2:76-80.

1977a   Worked bone tools 1976. In Hovenweep 1976, by Joseph C.
Winter. <u>San Jose State University archeological Report,
No.</u> 3:125-129.

1977b   Further studies of the potential faunal resources on Cajon Mesa. In Hovenweep 1976 by Joseph C. Winter. <u>San Jose State University Archeological Report, No. 3</u>:183-187.

1977c   An Analysis of the 1976 faunal remains. In Hovenweep 1976, by Joseph C. Winter. <u>San Jose State University Archeological Report, No. 3</u>:237-242.

Winter, Joseph C.
    1974   The Hovenweep Archaeological Project: a study of aboriginal agricultural patterns. <u>Southwestern Lore</u> 40(3 and 4):23-28.

    1975a   Hovenweep 1974. <u>San Jose State University Archaeological Report, No. 1</u>.

    1975b   Preliminary report: Hovenweep 1975. Bureau of Land Management, Montrose. xeroxed.

    1976a   Hovenweep 1976: preliminary report. Bureau of Land Management, Montrose. xeroxed.

    1976b   Hovenweep 1975. (2 Vols.) <u>San Jose State University Archaeological Report, No. 2</u>.

    1977   Hovenweep 1976. <u>San Jose State University Archeological Report, No. 3</u>.

Winter, Joseph C. and William J. Litzinger
    1976   Floral indicators of farm fields. In Hovenweep 1975, by Joseph C. Winger. <u>San Jose State University Archeological Report, No. 2</u>:123-168.

Winter, Joe, Laurel Casjens, Pat Hogan, and Brad Noisat
    1977   Site descriptions. In Hovenweep 1976, by Joseph C. Winter. <u>San Jose State University Archeological Report, No. 3</u>:10-62.

Wood, G. V. Kelly and A. MacAlpin
    1948   Geology of southern part of Archuleta County Colorado. United States Geological Survey Orland Gas Investigations, Preliminary Map 81. Portland, Oregon.

Wood, H. B.
    1938   Types of stone used for tools by the Mesa Verde Indians. <u>Mesa Verde Notes</u> 8(1):1-13.

Woodbury, Angus M.
    1961   Ecological studies of the flora and fauna of Navajo Reservoir Basin, Colorado and New Mexico. <u>University of Utah Anthropological Papers, No. 55</u>.

87

Woodbury, G.
1930   The Cliff Dwellers of Colorado. Discovery 12:278-82.
            Philadelphia.

1931   A preliminary note of the investigation of human hair.
            Colorado Magazine 8(2):47-48.

Woosley, Anne I.
1977   Farm field location through palynology. In Hovenweep
            1976, by Joseph C. Winter. San Jose State University
            Archeological Report, No. 3:133-150.

Wormington, H. M.
1947   Prehistoric Indians of the Southwest. Denver Museum of
            Natural History Popular Series, No. 7.

Wormington, H. m. and Arminta Neal
1951   The story of Pueblo pottery. Denver Museum of Natural
            History Museum Pictorial, No. 2.

Wyckoff, Don G.
1977   Secondary forest succession following abandonment of Mesa
            Verde. Kiva 42(3 and 4):215-231.

Yelm, Betty
1935a   Faces of the Mesa Verde people. Mesa Verde Notes 6(2):1-17.

1935b   Skull deformities of the Cliff Dweller. Mesa Verde Notes
            6(1):1-14.

Zier, Chris
1976   Analysis of edge wear on "projectile points" from
            Yellowjacket Colorado. Department of Anthropology,
            University of Colorado, Boulder. xeroxed.

1977   Prehistoric utilization of the House Creek drainage,
            San Juan National Forest, Colorado. Southwestern Lore
            43(2):1-11.

Zier, Christian J. and Christine Robinson
1975   Archaeological resources of the House Creek timber sale,
            San Juan National Forest Colorado. U.S. Forest Service,
            San Juan National Forest, Durango. xeroxed.

Zimmerman, Jorn
1970   Analysis of stone artifact forms and debris collected
            during the 1969 season on the Southern Ute Reservation.
            Department of Anthropology, University of Colorado,
            Boulder. xeroxed.

☙ U. S. GOVERNMENT PRINTING OFFICE 1978-777-356/301 Reg. 8

www.ingramcontent.com/pod-product-compliance
Lightning Source LLC
Chambersburg PA
CBHW080315290526
45790CB00005B/2049